DAILY BREAD:
Transformational Devotion for Men

Dr William C. Small

Daily Bread: Transformational Devotion for Men
Copyright © 2020 Dr William C. Small
All rights reserved under international copyright law.

FirstWorld Publishing
5000 Eldorado Parkway, Dallas, TX 75033
www.drwillspeaking.com

Contents may not be reproduced in whole or in part in any form or by any means whatsoever, whether electronic or mechanical (including information storage, recording, and retrieval systems) without express written consent from the publisher.

ISBN – 13: 9780997206777
ISBN – 10: 0997206772

Cover Photo: ©Istockphoto.com
Interior & cover design: FirstWorld Publishing

Unless otherwise indicated, all scripture quotations are from the King James Version of the Bible.

Scriptures were taken from the Thompson ChainReference Bible, Fifth Improved Edition, copyright © 1908, 1917, 1929, 1934, 1957, 1964, 1982, by Frank Charles Thompson.

Information within the verses of scripture contained in brackets [ ] was added by the author.

Hebrew and Greek definitions were taken from Strong's New Exhaustive Concordance Of The Bible, copyright © 1890, by

James Strong, STD,

LL.D. and cross referenced with Young's Analytical Concordance To The Bible, copyright © 1982, by Thomas Nelson, Inc.

Historical references were taken from Nelson's Illustrated Encyclopedia of Bible Facts, copyright © 1980 1995, by Thomas Nelson Publishers.

Please visit www.WealthBuilderSeminars.com or Amazon.com for other books by Dr. William Small.

Dedication

To my daughter **Deandra** and her generation

Contents

Preface	11
Section I	15
TRANSFORMATION	
Daily Devotion	
Day 1	17
Day 2	27
Day 3	39
Day 4	47
Day 5	61
Day 6	73
Day 7	85
Day 8	101
Day 9	117
Day 10	127
Day 11	139
Day 12	151
Day 13	161

Day 14	171
Day 15	187
Day 16	203
Day 17	221
Day 18	233
Day 19	249
Day 20	261
Day 21	271
Day 22	289
Day 23	307
Day 24	317
Day 25	343
Day 26	351
Day 27	359
Day 28	367
Day 29	381
Day 30	391
Day 31	401
Section II	405
Inspiration	
Motivation to Continue	

Daily Prayer	407
Keep the Change	413
Be Fruitful and Multiply	419
Can You be a Man Like Joseph ?	423
Section III	429
IN-FORMATION	
Transformation of the Heart and Mind	
The Truth about Perfection	431
The 7 Step Progression of Sin	435
Voice of GOD vs. Voice of Satan	441
Receive the Gifts of the Holy Spirit	449
The Question of a Man's Covering	455
About the Author	467

Preface

"...be not conformed to this world: but be you transformed by the renewing of your mind, that you may prove what is that good, and acceptable, and perfect, will of GOD. (Romans 12:2)."

Of course women can benefit from the daily devotion plan outlined in this book. However, Daily Bread: Transformational Devotion for Men endeavors to provide organization and structure to a man's time that he committed or dedicated to spend with GOD in the word of GOD. It divides Proverbs and Psalms into 31 day increments for men to read daily in an effort to sow the word of GOD in their hearts and transform their lives. Religion has made words like "devotion" seem spooky or something difficult to do. But devotion simply means being determined to dedicate a certain time and space in your home to spend in the presence of GOD everyday. Isaiah 43:26 says: "Put me in remembrance: let us plead together: declare you, that you may be justified." And Matthew 6:33 says that GOD already knows what you need. So, the thing that HE wants to hear when we spend time with HIM is HIS word. When you give voice to the HIS word GOD will give you power to transform your world and your increase wealth.

The word of GOD is a seed that will produce what GOD designed it to produce. An apple seed always produce an apple tree. Isaiah 55:1011 and Jeremiah 1:12c says that

Preface

GOD's word will not return to HIM void or it will always produce what HE intended and HE will hasten HIS word to make it produce quickly. Tress take time but when you sow the word in you it is designed to grow or produce quickly. Like John leaped in his mother's womb in the presence of Jesus (who is the word of GOD) the word can take a quantum leap inside of you to make you grow quickly.

Your body is comprised of primarily water and dirt. Seeds need water and dirt to grow. Seeds also need light in order to produce once they bud. John 1:45 says that the word of GOD is the light of the world and the light of men. The more light men receive the more the seeds of the word of GOD in them will have the power to produce. Men of GOD are able to produce on one of three levels: fruit, more fruit, or much fruit depending upon how much light they have or well they have been enlightened by the word. If you know the word you can produce fruit. If you are wise or diligently apply the word to your life you can produce more fruit. And if you apply the word to the point where you fully understand it, you can produce much fruit. Men of understanding receive the power of GOD to change things quickly and move things quantumly like timelapsed photography. Men of understanding can do all things bigger, better, and faster than other men because they have no obstacles blocking them.

If you read this book every day without fail for 3 years it will transform you into a man of understanding. 3 years will seem unreasonable to men who are still captives mentally to an instant oatmeal microwave society. However, men of understanding know that numbers in the Bible have power and significance. The number 3 for example represents divinity, 6 is represents man, and 9 represent victory. The number 9 is symbolic of a man who has achieved victory over himself. If you read this book diligently every day for 3 years you will have read through the books of Proverbs and Psalms 36 times. The number 36 is important because it will activate the power of quantum physics, quickly turn your life that is upside down right side up, and transform you spiritually. You see, man comes into the world upside down as a 6 with his head pointed away from GOD. Before a man can learn to walk with GOD as Adam did in the Garden he has to turn his head as a 9 back toward GOD. The number 36 is important because 3+6=9 or victory. Once a man (6) reaches divinity (3) he can achieve victory (9) over the obstacles within himself and in the world that keep him from receiving and walking in abundant blessings.

We hear men in their 50's proclaiming "GOD is not finished with me yet" to confess that they have not overcome their humanity. Some of them have been going to church regularly for decades but are still struggling in their humanity because nobody showed them how to reach divinity. Romans 12:12 instructs us to submit our bodies to GOD as a living sacrifice and to renew our minds to make it conform to the word of GOD. However, it also teaches that GOD is not going to transform us from humanity to divinity. We have a duty to transform our self. GOD said this transformation is our reasonable service or the least we can do for HIM to receive the abundant blessings HE has for us. The way that you transform your mind is though the washing of water by the word. The books of Proverbs and Psalms lead ordinary men to become extraordinary men. When your mind is renewed by the word in Psalms and Proverbs it will transform you from humanity to divinity. Then you can stand before GOD as kings and priests and have the power to operate in the dominion and authority over the world that HE gave you.

Finally, Psalms and Proverbs are located in the center or the heart of the Bible for a reason. The Bible teaches us how to have a vertical relationship with GOD and a horizontal relationship with mankind. Psalms shows us how to have a relationship with GOD and Proverbs shares the wisdom of GOD on how to have a relationship with each other. Psalms and Proverbs also provide a connection between the Old and New Testaments as well as serve as a witness to verify or confirm that the wisdom contained in those dispensations are true. The Bible is built on the principle of 2 or 3 witnesses so that it won't have to be interpreted by man's wisdom. The Bible was meant to be understood not interpreted. Psalms and Proverbs help you to understand the verses (or what GOD meant when HE said what HE said) so that you won't have to struggle to interpret them. If you spend enough time with GOD, HE will begin to tell you what HE meant when HE said what HE said.

Section I
TRANSFORMATION
Daily Devotion

Section I

Day 1

"For this is the covenant that I will make with the house of Israel after those days, saith the Lord; I will put my laws into their mind, and write them in their hearts: and I will be to them a GOD, and they shall be to me a people (Hebrews 8:10)."

If you read this devotional (Day 131) everyday for 3 years straight, the word of GOD will be written in your heart and mind. You will be able to understand the rest of the Bible more easily because Psalms and Proverbs are the center or heart of the Bible. The Bible is built on the two or three witness principle wherein GOD said: "out of the mouth of two or three witnesses let every word be established." This is why there are four gospels; each gospel has three witnesses to establish them. The verses in the books of Psalms and Proverbs serve as witnesses to verify or confirm other Bible verses.

Psalms 1

Blessed is the man that walketh not in the counsel of the ungodly, nor standeth in the way of sinners, nor sitteth in the seat of the scornful.

2 But his delight is in the law of the Lord; and in his law doth he meditate day and night.

Day 1

3 And he shall be like a tree planted by the rivers of water, that bringeth forth his fruit in his season; his leaf also shall not wither; and whatsoever he doeth shall prosper.

4 The ungodly are not so: but are like the chaff which the wind driveth away.

5 Therefore the ungodly shall not stand in the judgment, nor sinners in the congregation of the righteous.

6 For the Lord knoweth the way of the righteous: but the way of the ungodly shall perish.

Psalms 2

Why do the heathen rage, and the people imagine a vain thing?

2 The kings of the earth set themselves, and the rulers take counsel together, against the Lord, and against his anointed, saying,

3 Let us break their bands asunder, and cast away their cords from us.

4 He that sitteth in the heavens shall laugh: the Lord shall have them
in derision.

5 Then shall he speak unto them in his wrath, and vex them in his sore displeasure.

6 Yet have I set my king upon my holy hill of Zion.

7 I will declare the decree: the Lord hath said unto me, Thou art my Son; this day have I begotten thee.

8 Ask of me, and I shall give thee the heathen for thine inheritance, and the uttermost parts of the earth for thy possession.

9 Thou shalt break them with a rod of iron; thou shalt dash them in pieces like a potter's vessel.

10 Be wise now therefore, O ye kings: be instructed, ye judges of the earth.

11 Serve the Lord with fear, and rejoice with trembling.

12 Kiss the Son, lest he be angry, and ye perish from the way, when his wrath is kindled but a little. Blessed are all they that put their trust in him.

Psalms 3

Lord, how are they increased that trouble me! many are they that rise up against me.

2 Many there be which say of my soul, There is no help for him in GOD. Selah.

Day 1

3 But thou, O Lord, art a shield for me; my glory, and the lifter up of mine head.

4 I cried unto the Lord with my voice, and he heard me out of his holy hill. Selah.

5 I laid me down and slept; I awaked; for the Lord sustained me.

6 I will not be afraid of ten thousands of people, that have set themselves against me round about.

7 Arise, O Lord; save me, O my GOD: for thou hast smitten all mine enemies upon the cheek bone; thou hast broken the teeth of the ungodly.

8 Salvation belongeth unto the Lord: thy blessing is upon thy people. Selah.

Psalms 4

Hear me when I call, O GOD of my righteousness: thou hast enlarged me when I was in distress; have mercy upon me, and hear my prayer.

2 O ye sons of men, how long will ye turn my glory into shame? how long will ye love vanity, and seek after leasing? Selah.

3 But know that the Lord hath set apart him that is Godly for himself: the Lord will hear when I call unto him.

4 Stand in awe, and sin not: commune with your own heart upon your bed, and be still. Selah.

5 Offer the sacrifices of righteousness, and put your trust in the Lord.

6 There be many that say, Who will shew us any good? Lord, lift thou up the light of thy countenance upon us.

7 Thou hast put gladness in my heart, more than in the time that their corn and their wine increased.

8 I will both lay me down in peace, and sleep: for thou, Lord, only makest me dwell in safety.

Psalms 5

Give ear to my words, O Lord, consider my meditation.

2 Hearken unto the voice of my cry, my King, and my GOD: for unto thee will I pray.

3 My voice shalt thou hear in the morning, O Lord; in the morning will I direct my prayer unto thee, and will look up.

4 For thou art not a GOD that hath pleasure in wickedness: neither shall evil dwell with thee.

5 The foolish shall not stand in thy sight: thou hatest all workers of iniquity.

Day 1

6 Thou shalt destroy them that speak leasing: the Lord will abhor the bloody and deceitful man.

7 But as for me, I will come into thy house in the multitude of thy mercy: and in thy fear will I worship toward thy holy temple.

8 Lead me, O Lord, in thy righteousness because of mine enemies; make thy way straight before my face.

9 For there is no faithfulness in their mouth; their inward part is very wickedness; their throat is an open sepulchre; they flatter with their tongue.

10 Destroy thou them, O GOD; let them fall by their own counsels; cast them out in the multitude of their transgressions; for they have rebelled against thee.

11 But let all those that put their trust in thee rejoice: let them ever shout for joy, because thou defendest them: let them also that love thy name be joyful in thee.

12 For thou, Lord, wilt bless the righteous; with favour wilt thou compass him as with a shield.

Proverbs 1

The proverbs of Solomon the son of David, king of Israel;

2 To know wisdom and instruction; to perceive the words of understanding;

Day 1

3 To receive the instruction of wisdom, justice, and judgment, and equity;

4 To give subtilty to the simple, to the young man knowledge and discretion.

5 A wise man will hear, and will increase learning; and a man of understanding shall attain unto wise counsels:

6 To understand a proverb, and the interpretation; the words of the wise, and their dark sayings.

7 The fear of the Lord is the beginning of knowledge: but fools despise wisdom and instruction.

8 My son, hear the instruction of your father, and forsake not the law of your mother:

9 For they shall be an ornament of grace unto your head, and chains about your neck.

10 My son, if sinners entice thee, consent you not.

11 If they say, Come with us, let us lay wait for blood, let us lurk privily for the innocent without cause:

12 Let us swallow them up alive as the grave; and whole, as those that go down into the pit:

13 We shall find all precious substance, we shall fill our houses with spoil:

Day 1

14 Cast in your lot among us; let us all have one purse:

15 My son, walk not you in the way with them; refrain your foot from their path:

16 For their feet run to evil, and make haste to shed blood.

17 Surely in vain the net is spread in the sight of any bird.

18 And they lay wait for their own blood; they lurk privily for their own lives.

19 So are the ways of every one that is greedy of gain; which taketh away the life of the owners thereof.

20 Wisdom crieth without; she uttereth her voice in the streets:

21 She crieth in the chief place of concourse, in the openings of the gates: in the city she uttereth her words, saying,

22 How long, you simple ones, will you love simplicity? and the scorners delight in their scorning, and fools hate knowledge?

23 Turn you at my reproof: behold, I will pour out my spirit unto you, I will make known my words unto you.

24 Because I have called, and you refused; I have stretched out my hand, and no man regarded;

Day 1

25 But you have set at nought all my counsel, and would none of my reproof:

26 I also will laugh at your calamity; I will mock when your fear cometh;

27 When your fear cometh as desolation, and your destruction cometh as a whirlwind; when distress and anguish cometh upon you.

28 Then shall they call upon me, but I will not answer; they shall seek me early, but they shall not find me:

29 For that they hated knowledge, and did not choose the fear of the Lord:

30 They would none of my counsel: they despised all my reproof.

31 Therefore shall they eat of the fruit of their own way, and be filled with their own devices.

32 For the turning away of the simple shall slay them, and the prosperity of fools shall destroy them.

33 But whoso hearkeneth unto me shall dwell safely, and shall be quiet from fear of evil.

Day 1

Day 2

"Wherever GOD would build a church there would the devil also build a chapel." ~ Martin Luther

Psalms 6

O Lord, rebuke me not in thine anger, neither chasten me in thy hot displeasure.

2 Have mercy upon me, O Lord; for I am weak: O Lord, heal me; for my bones are vexed.

3 My soul is also sore vexed: but thou, O Lord, how long?

4 Return, O Lord, deliver my soul: oh save me for thy mercies' sake.

5 For in death there is no remembrance of thee: in the grave who shall give thee thanks?

6 I am weary with my groaning; all the night make I my bed to swim; I water my couch with my tears.

7 Mine eye is consumed because of grief; it waxeth old because of all mine enemies.

8 Depart from me, all ye workers of iniquity; for the Lord hath heard the voice of my weeping.

Day 2

9 The Lord hath heard my supplication; the Lord will receive my prayer.

10 Let all mine enemies be ashamed and sore vexed: let them return and be ashamed suddenly.

Psalms 7

O Lord my GOD, in thee do I put my trust: save me from all them that persecute me, and deliver me:

2 Lest he tear my soul like a lion, rending it in pieces, while there is none to deliver.

3 O Lord my GOD, If I have done this; if there be iniquity in my hands;

4 If I have rewarded evil unto him that was at peace with me; (yea, I have delivered him that without cause is mine enemy:)

5 Let the enemy persecute my soul, and take it; yea, let him tread down my life upon the earth, and lay mine honour in the dust. Selah.

6 Arise, O Lord, in thine anger, lift up thyself because of the rage of mine enemies: and awake for me to the judgment that thou hast commanded.

7 So shall the congregation of the people compass thee about: for their sakes therefore return thou on high.

8 The Lord shall judge the people: judge me, O Lord, according to my righteousness, and according to mine integrity that is in me.

9 Oh let the wickedness of the wicked come to an end; but establish the just: for the righteous GOD trieth the hearts and reins.

10 My defence is of GOD, which saveth the upright in heart.

11 GOD judgeth the righteous, and GOD is angry with the wicked every day.

12 If he turn not, he will whet his sword; he hath bent his bow, and made it ready.

13 He hath also prepared for him the instruments of death; he ordaineth his arrows against the persecutors.

14 Behold, he travaileth with iniquity, and hath conceived mischief, and brought forth falsehood.

15 He made a pit, and digged it, and is fallen into the ditch which he made.

16 His mischief shall return upon his own head, and his violent dealing shall come down upon his own pate.

17 I will praise the Lord according to his righteousness: and will sing praise to the name of the Lord most high.

Day 2

Psalms 8

O Lord, our Lord, how excellent is thy name in all the earth! who hast set thy glory above the heavens.

2 Out of the mouth of babes and sucklings hast thou ordained strength because of thine enemies, that thou mightest still the enemy and the avenger.

3 When I consider thy heavens, the work of thy fingers, the moon and the stars, which thou hast ordained;

4 What is man, that thou art mindful of him? and the son of man, that thou visitest him?

5 For thou hast made him a little lower than the angels, and hast crowned him with glory and honour.

6 Thou madest him to have dominion over the works of thy hands; thou hast put all things under his feet:

7 All sheep and oxen, yea, and the beasts of the field;

8 The fowl of the air, and the fish of the sea, and whatsoever passeth through the paths of the seas.

9 O Lord our Lord, how excellent is thy name in all the earth!

Psalms 9

I will praise thee, O Lord, with my whole heart; I will shew forth all thy marvellous works.

2 I will be glad and rejoice in thee: I will sing praise to thy name, O thou most High.

3 When mine enemies are turned back, they shall fall and perish at thy presence.

4 For thou hast maintained my right and my cause; thou satest in the throne judging right.

5 Thou hast rebuked the heathen, thou hast destroyed the wicked, thou hast put out their name for ever and ever.

6 O thou enemy, destructions are come to a perpetual end: and thou hast destroyed cities; their memorial is perished with them.

7 But the Lord shall endure for ever: he hath prepared his throne for judgment.

8 And he shall judge the world in righteousness, he shall minister judgment to the people in uprightness.

9 The Lord also will be a refuge for the oppressed, a refuge in times of trouble.

Day 2

10 And they that know thy name will put their trust in thee: for thou, Lord, hast not forsaken them that seek thee.

11 Sing praises to the Lord, which dwelleth in Zion: declare among the people his doings.

12 When he maketh inquisition for blood, he remembereth them: he forgetteth not the cry of the humble.

13 Have mercy upon me, O Lord; consider my trouble which I suffer of them that hate me, thou that liftest me up from the gates of death:

14 That I may shew forth all thy praise in the gates of the daughter of Zion: I will rejoice in thy salvation.

15 The heathen are sunk down in the pit that they made: in the net which they hid is their own foot taken.

16 The Lord is known by the judgment which he executeth: the wicked is snared in the work of his own hands. Higgaion. Selah.

17 The wicked shall be turned into hell, and all the nations that forget GOD.

18 For the needy shall not always be forgotten: the expectation of the poor shall not perish for ever.

19 Arise, O Lord; let not man prevail: let the heathen be judged in thy sight.

20 Put them in fear, O Lord: that the nations may know themselves to be but men. Selah.

Psalms 10

Why standest thou afar off, O Lord? why hidest thou thyself in times of trouble?

2 The wicked in his pride doth persecute the poor: let them be taken in the devices that they have imagined.

3 For the wicked boasteth of his heart's desire, and blesseth the covetous, whom the Lord abhorreth.

4 The wicked, through the pride of his countenance, will not seek after GOD: GOD is not in all his thoughts.

5 His ways are always grievous; thy judgments are far above out of his sight: as for all his enemies, he puffeth at them.

6 He hath said in his heart, I shall not be moved: for I shall never be in adversity.

7 His mouth is full of cursing and deceit and fraud: under his tongue is mischief and vanity.

8 He sitteth in the lurking places of the villages: in the secret places doth he murder the innocent: his eyes are privily set against the poor.

Day 2

9 He lieth in wait secretly as a lion in his den: he lieth in wait to catch the poor: he doth catch the poor, when he draweth him into his net.

10 He croucheth, and humbleth himself, that the poor may fall by his strong ones.

11 He hath said in his heart, GOD hath forgotten: he hideth his face; he will never see it.

12 Arise, O Lord; O GOD, lift up thine hand: forget not the humble.

13 Wherefore doth the wicked contemn GOD? he hath said in his heart, Thou wilt not require it.

14 Thou hast seen it; for thou beholdest mischief and spite, to requite it with thy hand: the poor committeth himself unto thee; thou art the helper of the fatherless.

15 Break thou the arm of the wicked and the evil man: seek out his wickedness till thou find none.

16 The Lord is King for ever and ever: the heathen are perished out of his land.

17 Lord, thou hast heard the desire of the humble: thou wilt prepare their heart, thou wilt cause thine ear to hear:

18 To judge the fatherless and the oppressed, that the man of the earth may no more oppress.

Proverbs 2

2 My son, if you wilt receive my words, and hide my commandments with thee;

2 So that you incline your ear unto wisdom, and apply your heart to understanding;

3 Yea, if you criest after knowledge, and liftest up your voice for understanding;

4 If you seekest her as silver, and searchest for her as for hid treasures;

5 Then shall you understand the fear of the Lord, and find the knowledge of GOD.

6 For the Lord giveth wisdom: out of his mouth cometh knowledge and understanding.

7 He layouth up sound wisdom for the righteous: he is a buckler to them that walk uprightly.

8 He keepeth the paths of judgment, and preserveth the way of his saints.

9 Then shall you understand righteousness, and judgment, and equity; yea, every good path.

10 When wisdom entereth into your heart, and knowledge is pleasant unto your soul;

Day 2

11 Discretion shall preserve thee, understanding shall keep thee:

12 To deliver thee from the way of the evil man, from the man that speaketh froward things;

13 Who leave the paths of uprightness, to walk in the ways of darkness;

14 Who rejoice to do evil, and delight in the frowardness of the wicked;

15 Whose ways are crooked, and they froward in their paths:

16 To deliver thee from the strange woman, even from the stranger which flattereth with her words;

17 Which forsaketh the guide of her youth, and forgetteth the covenant of her GOD.

18 For her house inclineth unto death, and her paths unto the dead.

19 None that go unto her return again, neither take they hold of the paths of life.

20 That you mayoust walk in the way of good men, and keep the paths of the righteous.

Day 2

21 For the upright shall dwell in the land, and the perfect shall remain in it.

22 But the wicked shall be cut off from the earth, and the transgressors shall be rooted out of it.

Day 2

Day 3

Psalms 11

In the Lord put I my trust: how say ye to my soul, Flee as a bird to your mountain?

2 For, lo, the wicked bend their bow, they make ready their arrow upon the string, that they may privily shoot at the upright in heart.

3 If the foundations be destroyed, what can the righteous do?

4 The Lord is in his holy temple, the Lord's throne is in heaven: his eyes behold, his eyelids try, the children of men.

5 The Lord trieth the righteous: but the wicked and him that loveth violence his soul hateth.

6 Upon the wicked he shall rain snares, fire and brimstone, and an horrible tempest: this shall be the portion of their cup.

7 For the righteous Lord loveth righteousness; his countenance doth behold the upright.

Day 3

Psalms 12

Help, Lord; for the Godly man ceaseth; for the faithful fail from among the children of men.

2 They speak vanity every one with his neighbour: with flattering lips and with a double heart do they speak.

3 The Lord shall cut off all flattering lips, and the tongue that speaketh proud things:

4 Who have said, With our tongue will we prevail; our lips are our own: who is lord over us?

5 For the oppression of the poor, for the sighing of the needy, now will I arise, saith the Lord; I will set him in safety from him that puffeth at him.

6 The words of the Lord are pure words: as silver tried in a furnace of earth, purified seven times.

7 Thou shalt keep them, O Lord, thou shalt preserve them from this generation for ever.

8 The wicked walk on every side, when the vilest men are exalted.

Psalms 13

How long wilt thou forget me, O Lord? for ever? how long wilt thou hide thy face from me?

2 How long shall I take counsel in my soul, having sorrow in my heart daily? how long shall mine enemy be exalted over me?

3 Consider and hear me, O Lord my GOD: lighten mine eyes, lest I sleep the sleep of death;

4 Lest mine enemy say, I have prevailed against him; and those that trouble me rejoice when I am moved.

5 But I have trusted in thy mercy; my heart shall rejoice in thy salvation.

6 I will sing unto the Lord, because he hath dealt bountifully with me.

Psalms 14

The fool hath said in his heart, There is no GOD. They are corrupt, they have done abominable works, there is none that doeth good.

2 The Lord looked down from heaven upon the children of men, to see if there were any that did understand, and seek GOD.

3 They are all gone aside, they are all together become filthy: there is none that doeth good, no, not one.

4 Have all the workers of iniquity no knowledge? who eat up my people as they eat bread, and call not upon the Lord.

5 There were they in great fear: for GOD is in the generation of the righteous.

6 Ye have shamed the counsel of the poor, because the Lord is his refuge.

7 Oh that the salvation of Israel were come out of Zion! when the Lord bringeth back the captivity of his people, Jacob shall rejoice,

and Israel shall be glad.

Psalms 15

Lord, who shall abide in thy tabernacle? who shall dwell in thy holy hill?

2 He that walketh uprightly, and worketh righteousness, and speaketh the truth in his heart.

3 He that backbiteth not with his tongue, nor doeth evil to his neighbour, nor taketh up a reproach against his neighbour.

4 In whose eyes a vile person is contemned; but he honoureth them that fear the Lord. He that sweareth to his own hurt, and changeth not.

5 He that putteth not out his money to usury, nor taketh reward against the innocent. He that doeth these things shall never be moved.

Proverbs 3

My son, forget not my law; but let your heart keep my commandments:

2 For length of days, and long life, and peace, shall they add to thee.

3 Let not mercy and truth forsake thee: bind them about your neck; write them upon the table of your heart:

4 So shall you find favour and good understanding in the sight of GOD and man.

5 Trust in the Lord with all your heart; and lean not unto your own understanding.

6 In all your ways acknowledge him, and he shall direct your paths.

7 Be not wise in your own eyes: fear the Lord, and depart from evil.

8 It shall be health to your navel, and marrow to your bones.

9 Honour the Lord with your substance, and with the firstfruits of all your increase:

10 So shall your barns be filled with plenty, and your presses shall burst out with new wine.

Day 3

11 My son, despise not the chastening of the Lord; neither be weary of his correction:

12 For whom the Lord loveth he correcteth; even as a father the son in whom he delighteth.

13 Happy is the man that findeth wisdom, and the man that getteth understanding.

14 For the merchandise of it is better than the merchandise of silver, and the gain thereof than fine gold.

15 She is more precious than rubies: and all the things you canst desire are not to be compared unto her.

16 Length of days is in her right hand; and in her left hand riches and honour.

17 Her ways are ways of pleasantness, and all her paths are peace.

18 She is a tree of life to them that lay hold upon her: and happy is every one that retaineth her.

19 The Lord by wisdom has founded the earth; by understanding has he established the heavens.

20 By his knowledge the depths are broken up, and the clouds drop down the dew.

21 My son, let not them depart from your eyes: keep sound wisdom and discretion:

22 So shall they be life unto your soul, and grace to your neck.

23 Then shall you walk in your way safely, and your foot shall not stumble.

24 When you liest down, you shall not be afraid: yea, you shall lie down, and your sleep shall be sweet.

25 Be not afraid of sudden fear, neither of the desolation of the wicked, when it cometh.

26 For the Lord shall be your confidence, and shall keep your foot from being taken.

27 Withhold not good from them to whom it is due, when it is in the power of your hand to do it.

28 Say not unto your neighbour, Go, and come again, and to morrow I will give; when you hast it by thee.

29 Devise not evil against your neighbour, seeing he dwelleth securely by thee.

30 Strive not with a man without cause, if he have done thee no harm.

Day 3

31 Envy you not the oppressor, and choose none of his ways.

32 For the froward is abomination to the Lord: but his secret is with the righteous.

33 The curse of the Lord is in the house of the wicked: but he blesseth the habitation of the just.

34 Surely he scorneth the scorners: but he giveth grace unto the lowly.

35 The wise shall inherit glory: but shame shall be the promotion of fools.

Day 4

"Crisis is always a prelude to opportunity." ~ Dr Will

Psalms 16

Preserve me, O GOD: for in thee do I put my trust.

2 O my soul, thou hast said unto the Lord, Thou art my Lord: my goodness extendeth not to thee;

3 But to the saints that are in the earth, and to the excellent, in whom is all my delight.

4 Their sorrows shall be multiplied that hasten after another GOD: their drink offerings of blood will I not offer, nor take up their names into my lips.

5 The Lord is the portion of mine inheritance and of my cup: thou maintainest my lot.

6 The lines are fallen unto me in pleasant places; yea, I have a goodly heritage.

7 I will bless the Lord, who hath given me counsel: my reins also instruct me in the night seasons.

8 I have set the Lord always before me: because he is at my right hand, I shall not be moved.

9 Therefore my heart is glad, and my glory rejoiceth: my flesh also shall rest in hope.

10 For thou wilt not leave my soul in hell; neither wilt thou suffer thine Holy One to see corruption.

11 Thou wilt shew me the path of life: in thy presence is fulness of joy; at thy right hand there are pleasures for evermore.

Psalms 17

Hear the right, O Lord, attend unto my cry, give ear unto my prayer, that goeth not out of feigned lips.

2 Let my sentence come forth from thy presence; let thine eyes behold the things that are equal.

3 Thou hast proved mine heart; thou hast visited me in the night; thou hast tried me, and shalt find nothing; I am purposed that my mouth shall not transgress.

4 Concerning the works of men, by the word of thy lips I have kept me from the paths of the destroyer.

5 Hold up my goings in thy paths, that my footsteps slip not.

6 I have called upon thee, for thou wilt hear me, O GOD: incline thine ear unto me, and hear my speech.

Day 4

7 Shew thy marvellous lovingkindness, O thou that savest by thy right hand them which put their trust in thee from those that rise up against them.

8 Keep me as the apple of the eye, hide me under the shadow of thy wings,

9 From the wicked that oppress me, from my deadly enemies, who compass me about.

10 They are inclosed in their own fat: with their mouth they speak proudly.

11 They have now compassed us in our steps: they have set their eyes bowing down to the earth;

12 Like as a lion that is greedy of his prey, and as it were a young lion lurking in secret places.

13 Arise, O Lord, disappoint him, cast him down: deliver my soul from the wicked, which is thy sword:

14 From men which are thy hand, O Lord, from men of the world, which have their portion in this life, and whose belly thou fillest with thy hid treasure: they are full of children, and leave the rest of their substance to their babes.

15 As for me, I will behold thy face in righteousness: I shall be satisfied, when I awake, with thy likeness.

Day 4

Psalms 18

I will love thee, O Lord, my strength.

2 The Lord is my rock, and my fortress, and my deliverer; my GOD, my strength, in whom I will trust; my buckler, and the horn of my salvation, and my high tower.

3 I will call upon the Lord, who is worthy to be praised: so shall I be saved from mine enemies.

4 The sorrows of death compassed me, and the floods of ungodly men made me afraid.

5 The sorrows of hell compassed me about: the snares of death prevented me.

6 In my distress I called upon the Lord, and cried unto my GOD: he heard my voice out of his temple, and my cry came before him, even into his ears.

7 Then the earth shook and trembled; the foundations also of the hills moved and were shaken, because he was wroth.

8 There went up a smoke out of his nostrils, and fire out of his mouth devoured: coals were kindled by it.

9 He bowed the heavens also, and came down: and darkness was under his feet.

10 And he rode upon a cherub, and did fly: yea, he did fly upon the wings of the wind.

11 He made darkness his secret place; his pavilion round about him were dark waters and thick clouds of the skies.

12 At the brightness that was before him his thick clouds passed, hail stones and coals of fire.

13 The Lord also thundered in the heavens, and the Highest gave his voice; hail stones and coals of fire.

14 Yea, he sent out his arrows, and scattered them; and he shot out lightnings, and discomfited them.

15 Then the channels of waters were seen, and the foundations of the world were discovered at thy rebuke, O Lord, at the blast of the breath of thy nostrils.

16 He sent from above, he took me, he drew me out of many waters.

17 He delivered me from my strong enemy, and from them which hated me: for they were too strong for me.

18 They prevented me in the day of my calamity: but the Lord was my stay.

19 He brought me forth also into a large place; he delivered me, because he delighted in me.

Day 4

20 The Lord rewarded me according to my righteousness; according to the cleanness of my hands hath he recompensed me.

21 For I have kept the ways of the Lord, and have not wickedly departed from my GOD.

22 For all his judgments were before me, and I did not put away his statutes from me.

23 I was also upright before him, and I kept myself from mine iniquity.

24 Therefore hath the Lord recompensed me according to my righteousness, according to the cleanness of my hands in his eyesight.

25 With the merciful thou wilt shew thyself merciful; with an upright man thou wilt shew thyself upright;

26 With the pure thou wilt shew thyself pure; and with the froward thou wilt shew thyself froward.

27 For thou wilt save the afflicted people; but wilt bring down high looks.

28 For thou wilt light my candle: the Lord my GOD will enlighten my darkness.

29 For by thee I have run through a troop; and by my GOD have I leaped over a wall.

Day 4

30 As for GOD, his way is perfect: the word of the Lord is tried: he is a buckler to all those that trust in him.

31 For who is GOD save the Lord? or who is a rock save our GOD?

32 It is GOD that girdeth me with strength, and maketh my way perfect.

33 He maketh my feet like hinds' feet, and setteth me upon my high places.

34 He teacheth my hands to war, so that a bow of steel is broken by mine arms.

35 Thou hast also given me the shield of thy salvation: and thy right hand hath holden me up, and thy gentleness hath made me great.

36 Thou hast enlarged my steps under me, that my feet did not slip.

37 I have pursued mine enemies, and overtaken them: neither did I turn again till they were consumed.

38 I have wounded them that they were not able to rise: they are fallen under my feet.

39 For thou hast girded me with strength unto the battle: thou hast subdued under me those that rose up against me.

Day 4

40 Thou hast also given me the necks of mine enemies; that I might destroy them that hate me.

41 They cried, but there was none to save them: even unto the Lord, but he answered them not.

42 Then did I beat them small as the dust before the wind: I did cast them out as the dirt in the streets.

43 Thou hast delivered me from the strivings of the people; and thou hast made me the head of the heathen: a people whom I have not known shall serve me.

44 As soon as they hear of me, they shall obey me: the strangers shall submit themselves unto me.

45 The strangers shall fade away, and be afraid out of their close places.

46 The Lord liveth; and blessed be my rock; and let the GOD of my salvation be exalted.

47 It is GOD that avengeth me, and subdueth the people under me.

48 He delivereth me from mine enemies: yea, thou liftest me up above those that rise up against me: thou hast delivered me from the violent man.

49 Therefore will I give thanks unto thee, O Lord, among the heathen, and sing praises unto thy name.

50 Great deliverance giveth he to his king; and sheweth mercy to his anointed, to David, and to his seed for evermore.

Psalms 19

The heavens declare the glory of GOD; and the firmament sheweth his handywork.

2 Day unto day uttereth speech, and night unto night sheweth knowledge.

3 There is no speech nor language, where their voice is not heard.

4 Their line is gone out through all the earth, and their words to the end of the world. In them hath he set a tabernacle for the sun,

5 Which is as a bridegroom coming out of his chamber, and rejoiceth as a strong man to run a race.

6 His going forth is from the end of the heaven, and his circuit unto the ends of it: and there is nothing hid from the heat thereof.

7 The law of the Lord is perfect, converting the soul: the testimony of the Lord is sure, making wise the simple.

8 The statutes of the Lord are right, rejoicing the heart: the commandment of the Lord is pure, enlightening the eyes.

Day 4

9 The fear of the Lord is clean, enduring for ever: the judgments of the Lord are true and righteous altogether.

10 More to be desired are they than gold, yea, than much fine gold: sweeter also than honey and the honeycomb.

11 Moreover by them is thy servant warned: and in keeping of them there is great reward.

12 Who can understand his errors? cleanse thou me from secret faults.

13 Keep back thy servant also from presumptuous sins; let them not have dominion over me: then shall I be upright, and I shall be innocent from the great transgression.

14 Let the words of my mouth, and the meditation of my heart, be acceptable in thy sight, O Lord, my strength, and my redeemer.

Psalms 20

The Lord hear thee in the day of trouble; the name of the GOD of Jacob defend thee;

2 Send thee help from the sanctuary, and strengthen thee out of Zion;

3 Remember all thy offerings, and accept thy burnt sacrifice; Selah.

4 Grant thee according to thine own heart, and fulfil all thy counsel.

5 We will rejoice in thy salvation, and in the name of our GOD we will set up our banners: the Lord fulfil all thy petitions.

6 Now know I that the Lord saveth his anointed; he will hear him from his holy heaven with the saving strength of his right hand.

7 Some trust in chariots, and some in horses: but we will remember the name of the Lord our GOD.

8 They are brought down and fallen: but we are risen, and stand upright.

9 Save, Lord: let the king hear us when we call.

Proverbs 4

Hear, you children, the instruction of a father, and attend to know understanding.

2 For I give you good doctrine, forsake you not my law.

3 For I was my father's son, tender and only beloved in the sight of my mother.

4 He taught me also, and said unto me, Let your heart retain my words: keep my commandments, and live.

Day 4

5 Get wisdom, get understanding: forget it not; neither decline from the words of my mouth.

6 Forsake her not, and she shall preserve thee: love her, and she shall keep thee.

7 Wisdom is the principal thing; therefore get wisdom: and with all your getting get understanding.

8 Exalt her, and she shall promote thee: she shall bring thee to honour, when you dost embrace her.

9 She shall give to your head an ornament of grace: a crown of glory shall she deliver to thee.

10 Hear, O my son, and receive my sayings; and the years of your life shall be many.

11 I have taught thee in the way of wisdom; I have led thee in right paths.

12 When you goest, your steps shall not be straitened; and when you runnest, you shall not stumble.

13 Take fast hold of instruction; let her not go: keep her; for she is your life.

14 Enter not into the path of the wicked, and go not in the way of evil men.

15 Avoid it, pass not by it, turn from it, and pass away.

16 For they sleep not, except they have done mischief; and their sleep is taken away, unless they cause some to fall.

17 For they eat the bread of wickedness, and drink the wine of violence.

18 But the path of the just is as the shining light, that shineth more and more unto the perfect day.

19 The way of the wicked is as darkness: they know not at what they stumble.

20 My son, attend to my words; incline your ear unto my sayings.

21 Let them not depart from your eyes; keep them in the midst of your heart.

22 For they are life unto those that find them, and health to all their flesh.

23 Keep your heart with all diligence; for out of it are the issues of life.

24 Put away from thee a froward mouth, and perverse lips put far from thee.

25 Let your eyes look right on, and let your eyelids look straight before thee.

Day 4

26 Ponder the path of your feet, and let all your ways be established.

27 Turn not to the right hand nor to the left: remove your foot from evil.

Day 5

"Jesus cannot return as the King of Kings unless men become the Kings that we were meant to be." ~ Dr Will

Psalms 21

The king shall joy in thy strength, O Lord; and in thy salvation how greatly shall he rejoice!

2 Thou hast given him his heart's desire, and hast not withholden the request of his lips. Selah.

3 For thou preventest him with the blessings of goodness: thou settest a crown of pure gold on his head.

4 He asked life of thee, and thou gavest it him, even length of days for ever and ever.

5 His glory is great in thy salvation: honour and majesty hast thou laid upon him.

6 For thou hast made him most blessed for ever: thou hast made him exceeding glad with thy countenance.

7 For the king trusteth in the Lord, and through the mercy of the most High he shall not be moved.

8 Thine hand shall find out all thine enemies: thy right hand shall find out those that hate thee.

9 Thou shalt make them as a fiery oven in the time of thine anger: the Lord shall swallow them up in his wrath, and the fire shall devour them.

10 Their fruit shalt thou destroy from the earth, and their seed from among the children of men.

11 For they intended evil against thee: they imagined a mischievous device, which they are not able to perform.

12 Therefore shalt thou make them turn their back, when thou shalt make ready thine arrows upon thy strings against the face of them.

13 Be thou exalted, Lord, in thine own strength: so will we sing and praise thy power.

Psalms 22

My GOD, my GOD, why hast thou forsaken me? why art thou so far from helping me, and from the words of my roaring?

2 O my GOD, I cry in the day time, but thou hearest not; and in the night season, and am not silent.

3 But thou art holy, O thou that inhabitest the praises of Israel.

Day 5

4 Our fathers trusted in thee: they trusted, and thou didst deliver them.

5 They cried unto thee, and were delivered: they trusted in thee, and were not confounded.

6 But I am a worm, and no man; a reproach of men, and despised of the people.

7 All they that see me laugh me to scorn: they shoot out the lip, they shake the head, saying,

8 He trusted on the Lord that he would deliver him: let him deliver him, seeing he delighted in him.

9 But thou art he that took me out of the womb: thou didst make me hope when I was upon my mother's breasts.

10 I was cast upon thee from the womb: thou art my GOD from my mother's belly.

11 Be not far from me; for trouble is near; for there is none to help.

12 Many bulls have compassed me: strong bulls of Bashan have beset me round.

13 They gaped upon me with their mouths, as a ravening and a roaring lion.

Day 5

14 I am poured out like water, and all my bones are out of joint: my heart is like wax; it is melted in the midst of my bowels.

15 My strength is dried up like a potsherd; and my tongue cleaveth to my jaws; and thou hast brought me into the dust of death.

16 For dogs have compassed me: the assembly of the wicked have inclosed me: they pierced my hands and my feet.

17 I may tell all my bones: they look and stare upon me.

18 They part my garments among them, and cast lots upon my vesture.

19 But be not thou far from me, O Lord: O my strength, haste thee to help me.

20 Deliver my soul from the sword; my darling from the power of the dog.

21 Save me from the lion's mouth: for thou hast heard me from the horns of the unicorns.

22 I will declare thy name unto my brethren: in the midst of the congregation will I praise thee.

23 Ye that fear the Lord, praise him; all ye the seed of Jacob, glorify him; and fear him, all ye the seed of Israel.

24 For he hath not despised nor abhorred the affliction of the afflicted; neither hath he hid his face from him; but when he cried unto him, he heard.

25 My praise shall be of thee in the great congregation: I will pay my vows before them that fear him.

26 The meek shall eat and be satisfied: they shall praise the Lord that seek him: your heart shall live for ever.

27 All the ends of the world shall remember and turn unto the Lord: and all the kindreds of the nations shall worship before thee.

28 For the kingdom is the Lord's: and he is the governor among the nations.

29 All they that be fat upon earth shall eat and worship: all they that go down to the dust shall bow before him: and none can keep alive his own soul.

30 A seed shall serve him; it shall be accounted to the Lord for a generation.

31 They shall come, and shall declare his righteousness unto a people that shall be born, that he hath done this.

Psalms 23

The Lord is my shepherd; I shall not want.

Day 5

2 He maketh me to lie down in green pastures: he leadeth me beside the still waters.

3 He restoreth my soul: he leadeth me in the paths of righteousness for his name's sake.

4 Yea, though I walk through the valley of the shadow of death, I will fear no evil: for thou art with me; thy rod and thy staff they comfort me.

5 Thou preparest a table before me in the presence of mine enemies: thou anointest my head with oil; my cup runneth over.

6 Surely goodness and mercy shall follow me all the days of my life: and I will dwell in the house of the Lord for ever.

Psalms 24

The earth is the Lord's, and the fulness thereof; the world, and they that dwell therein.

2 For he hath founded it upon the seas, and established it upon the floods.

3 Who shall ascend into the hill of the Lord? or who shall stand in his holy place?

4 He that hath clean hands, and a pure heart; who hath not lifted up his soul unto vanity, nor sworn deceitfully.

5 He shall receive the blessing from the Lord, and righteousness from the GOD of his salvation.

6 This is the generation of them that seek him, that seek thy face, O Jacob. Selah.

7 Lift up your heads, O ye gates; and be ye lift up, ye everlasting doors; and the King of glory shall come in.

8 Who is this King of glory? The Lord strong and mighty, the Lord mighty in battle.

9 Lift up your heads, O ye gates; even lift them up, ye everlasting doors; and the King of glory shall come in.

10 Who is this King of glory? The Lord of hosts, he is the King of glory. Selah.

Psalms 25

Unto thee, O Lord, do I lift up my soul.

2 O my GOD, I trust in thee: let me not be ashamed, let not mine enemies triumph over me.

3 Yea, let none that wait on thee be ashamed: let them be ashamed which transgress without cause.

4 Shew me thy ways, O Lord; teach me thy paths.

Day 5

5 Lead me in thy truth, and teach me: for thou art the GOD of my salvation; on thee do I wait all the day.

6 Remember, O Lord, thy tender mercies and thy lovingkindnesses; for they have been ever of old.

7 Remember not the sins of my youth, nor my transgressions: according to thy mercy remember thou me for thy goodness' sake, O Lord.

8 Good and upright is the Lord: therefore will he teach sinners in the way.

9 The meek will he guide in judgment: and the meek will he teach his way.

10 All the paths of the Lord are mercy and truth unto such as keep his covenant and his testimonies.

11 For thy name's sake, O Lord, pardon mine iniquity; for it is great.

12 What man is he that feareth the Lord? him shall he teach in the way that he shall choose.

13 His soul shall dwell at ease; and his seed shall inherit the earth.

14 The secret of the Lord is with them that fear him; and he will shew them his covenant.

15 Mine eyes are ever toward the Lord; for he shall pluck my feet out of the net.

16 Turn thee unto me, and have mercy upon me; for I am desolate and afflicted.

17 The troubles of my heart are enlarged: O bring thou me out of my distresses.

18 Look upon mine affliction and my pain; and forgive all my sins.

19 Consider mine enemies; for they are many; and they hate me with cruel hatred.

20 O keep my soul, and deliver me: let me not be ashamed; for I put my trust in thee.

21 Let integrity and uprightness preserve me; for I wait on thee.

22 Redeem Israel, O GOD, out of all his troubles.

Proverbs 5

My son, attend unto my wisdom, and bow your ear to my understanding:

2 That you mayoust regard discretion, and that your lips may keep knowledge.

Day 5

3 For the lips of a strange woman drop as an honeycomb, and her mouth is smoother than oil:

4 But her end is bitter as wormwood, sharp as a twoedged sword.

5 Her feet go down to death; her steps take hold on hell.

6 Lest you shouldest ponder the path of life, her ways are moveable, that you canst not know them.

7 Hear me now therefore, O you children, and depart not from the words of my mouth.

8 Remove your way far from her, and come not nigh the door of her house:

9 Lest you give your honour unto others, and your years unto the cruel:

10 Lest strangers be filled with your wealth; and your labours be in the house of a stranger;

11 And you mourn at the last, when your flesh and your body are consumed,

12 And say, How have I hated instruction, and my heart despised reproof;

13 And have not obeyed the voice of my teachers, nor inclined mine ear to them that instructed me!

Day 5

14 I was almost in all evil in the midst of the congregation and assembly.

15 Drink waters out of your own cistern, and running waters out of your own well.

16 Let your fountains be dispersed abroad, and rivers of waters in the streets.

17 Let them be only your own, and not strangers' with thee.

18 Let your fountain be blessed: and rejoice with the wife of your youth.

19 Let her be as the loving hind and pleasant roe; let her breasts satisfy thee at all times; and be you ravished always with her love.

20 And why wilt you, my son, be ravished with a strange woman, and embrace the bosom of a stranger?

21 For the ways of man are before the eyes of the Lord, and he pondereth all his goings.

22 His own iniquities shall take the wicked himself, and he shall be holden with the cords of his sins.

23 He shall die without instruction; and in the greatness of his folly he shall go astray.

Day 5

Day 6

"Integrity, like trust, is more easily kept than recovered."
~ Dr Will

Psalms 26

Judge me, O Lord; for I have walked in mine integrity: I have trusted also in the Lord; therefore I shall not slide.

2 Examine me, O Lord, and prove me; try my reins and my heart.

3 For thy lovingkindness is before mine eyes: and I have walked in thy truth.

4 I have not sat with vain persons, neither will I go in with dissemblers.

5 I have hated the congregation of evil doers; and will not sit with the wicked.

6 I will wash mine hands in innocency: so will I compass thine altar, O Lord:

7 That I may publish with the voice of thanksgiving, and tell of all thy wondrous works.

Day 6

8 Lord, I have loved the habitation of thy house, and the place where thine honour dwelleth.

9 Gather not my soul with sinners, nor my life with bloody men:

10 In whose hands is mischief, and their right hand is full of bribes.

11 But as for me, I will walk in mine integrity: redeem me, and be merciful unto me.

12 My foot standeth in an even place: in the congregations will I bless the Lord.

Psalms 27

The Lord is my light and my salvation; whom shall I fear? the Lord is the strength of my life; of whom shall I be afraid?

2 When the wicked, even mine enemies and my foes, came upon me to eat up my flesh, they stumbled and fell.

3 Though an host should encamp against me, my heart shall not fear: though war should rise against me, in this will I be confident.

4 One thing have I desired of the Lord, that will I seek after; that I may dwell in the house of the Lord all the days of my

life, to behold the beauty of the Lord, and to enquire in his temple.

5 For in the time of trouble he shall hide me in his pavilion: in the secret of his tabernacle shall he hide me; he shall set me up upon a rock.

6 And now shall mine head be lifted up above mine enemies round about me: therefore will I offer in his tabernacle sacrifices of joy; I will sing, yea, I will sing praises unto the Lord.

7 Hear, O Lord, when I cry with my voice: have mercy also upon me, and answer me.

8 When thou saidst, Seek ye my face; my heart said unto thee, Thy face, Lord, will I seek.

9 Hide not thy face far from me; put not thy servant away in anger: thou hast been my help; leave me not, neither forsake me, O GOD of my salvation.

10 When my father and my mother forsake me, then the Lord will take me up.

11 Teach me thy way, O Lord, and lead me in a plain path, because of mine enemies.

12 Deliver me not over unto the will of mine enemies: for false witnesses are risen up against me, and such as breathe out cruelty.

13 I had fainted, unless I had believed to see the goodness of the Lord in the land of the living.

14 Wait on the Lord: be of good courage, and he shall strengthen thine heart: wait, I say, on the Lord.

Psalms 28

Unto thee will I cry, O Lord my rock; be not silent to me: lest, if thou be silent to me, I become like them that go down into the pit.

2 Hear the voice of my supplications, when I cry unto thee, when I lift up my hands toward thy holy oracle.

3 Draw me not away with the wicked, and with the workers of iniquity, which speak peace to their neighbours, but mischief is in their hearts.

4 Give them according to their deeds, and according to the wickedness of their endeavours: give them after the work of their hands; render to them their desert.

5 Because they regard not the works of the Lord, nor the operation of his hands, he shall destroy them, and not build them up.

6 Blessed be the Lord, because he hath heard the voice of my supplications.

7 The Lord is my strength and my shield; my heart trusted in him, and I am helped: therefore my heart greatly rejoiceth; and with my song will I praise him.

8 The Lord is their strength, and he is the saving strength of his anointed.

9 Save thy people, and bless thine inheritance: feed them also, and lift them up for ever.

Psalms 29

Give unto the Lord, O ye mighty, give unto the Lord glory and strength.

2 Give unto the Lord the glory due unto his name; worship the Lord in the beauty of holiness.

3 The voice of the Lord is upon the waters: the GOD of glory thundereth: the Lord is upon many waters.

4 The voice of the Lord is powerful; the voice of the Lord is full of majesty.

5 The voice of the Lord breaketh the cedars; yea, the Lord breaketh the cedars of Lebanon.

6 He maketh them also to skip like a calf; Lebanon and Sirion like a young unicorn.

7 The voice of the Lord divideth the flames of fire.

Day 6

8 The voice of the Lord shaketh the wilderness; the Lord shaketh the wilderness of Kadesh.

9 The voice of the Lord maketh the hinds to calve, and discovereth the forests: and in his temple doth every one speak of his glory.

10 The Lord sitteth upon the flood; yea, the Lord sitteth King for ever.

11 The Lord will give strength unto his people; the Lord will bless his people with peace.

Psalms 30

I will extol thee, O Lord; for thou hast lifted me up, and hast not made my foes to rejoice over me.

2 O Lord my GOD, I cried unto thee, and thou hast healed me.

3 O Lord, thou hast brought up my soul from the grave: thou hast kept me alive, that I should not go down to the pit.

4 Sing unto the Lord, O ye saints of his, and give thanks at the remembrance of his holiness.

5 For his anger endureth but a moment; in his favour is life: weeping may endure for a night, but joy cometh in the morning.

6 And in my prosperity I said, I shall never be moved.

7 Lord, by thy favour thou hast made my mountain to stand strong: thou didst hide thy face, and I was troubled.

8 I cried to thee, O Lord; and unto the Lord I made supplication.

9 What profit is there in my blood, when I go down to the pit? Shall the dust praise thee? shall it declare thy truth?

10 Hear, O Lord, and have mercy upon me: Lord, be thou my helper.

11 Thou hast turned for me my mourning into dancing: thou hast put off my sackcloth, and girded me with gladness;

12 To the end that my glory may sing praise to thee, and not be silent. O Lord my GOD, I will give thanks unto thee for ever.

Proverbs 6

My son, if you be surety for your friend, if you hast stricken your hand with a stranger,

2 You art snared with the words of your mouth, you art taken with the words of your mouth.

Day 6

3 Do this now, my son, and deliver yourself, when you art come into the hand of your friend; go, humble yourself, and make sure your friend.

4 Give not sleep to your eyes, nor slumber to your eyelids.

5 Deliver yourself as a roe from the hand of the hunter, and as a bird from the hand of the fowler.

6 Go to the ant, you sluggard; consider her ways, and be wise:

7 Which having no guide, overseer, or ruler,

8 Provideth her meat in the summer, and gathereth her food in the harvest.

9 How long wilt you sleep, O sluggard? when wilt you arise out of your sleep?

10 Yout a little sleep, a little slumber, a little folding of the hands to sleep:

11 So shall your poverty come as one that travelleth, and your want as an armed man.

12 A naughty person, a wicked man, walketh with a froward mouth.

13 He winketh with his eyes, he speaketh with his feet, he teacheth with his fingers;

Day 6

14 Frowardness is in his heart, he deviseth mischief continually; he soweth discord.

15 Therefore shall his calamity come suddenly; suddenly shall he be broken without remedy.

16 These six things doth the Lord hate: yea, seven are an abomination unto him:

17 A proud look, a lying tongue, and hands that shed innocent blood,

18 An heart that deviseth wicked imaginations, feet that be swift in running to mischief,

19 A false witness that speaketh lies, and he that soweth discord among brethren.

20 My son, keep your father's commandment, and forsake not the law of your mother:

21 Bind them continually upon your heart, and tie them about your neck.

22 When you goest, it shall lead thee; when you sleepest, it shall keep thee; and when you awakest, it shall talk with thee.

23 For the commandment is a lamp; and the law is light; and reproofs of instruction are the way of life:

Day 6

24 To keep thee from the evil woman, from the flattery of the tongue of a strange woman.

25 Lust not after her beauty in your heart; neither let her take thee with her eyelids.

26 For by means of a whorish woman a man is brought to a piece of bread: and the adultress will hunt for the precious life.

27 Can a man take fire in his bosom, and his clothes not be burned?

28 Can one go upon hot coals, and his feet not be burned?

29 So he that goeth in to his neighbour's wife; whosoever toucheth her shall not be innocent.

30 Men do not despise a thief, if he steal to satisfy his soul when he is hungry;

31 But if he be found, he shall restore sevenfold; he shall give all the substance of his house.

32 But whoso committeth adultery with a woman lacketh understanding: he that doeth it destroyouth his own soul.

33 A wound and dishonour shall he get; and his reproach shall not be wiped away.

34 For jealousy is the rage of a man: therefore he will not spare in the day of vengeance.

35 He will not regard any ransom; neither will he rest content, yough you givest many gifts.

Day 6

Day 7

"It is common for those that are farthest from GOD to boast themselves most of their being near to the church."
~ Matthew Henry

Psalms 31

In thee, O Lord, do I put my trust; let me never be ashamed: deliver me in thy righteousness.

2 Bow down thine ear to me; deliver me speedily: be thou my strong rock, for an house of defence to save me.

3 For thou art my rock and my fortress; therefore for thy name's sake lead me, and guide me.

4 Pull me out of the net that they have laid privily for me: for thou art my strength.

5 Into thine hand I commit my spirit: thou hast redeemed me, O Lord GOD of truth.

6 I have hated them that regard lying vanities: but I trust in the Lord.

7 I will be glad and rejoice in thy mercy: for thou hast considered my trouble; thou hast known my soul in adversities;

8 And hast not shut me up into the hand of the enemy: thou hast set my feet in a large room.

9 Have mercy upon me, O Lord, for I am in trouble: mine eye is consumed with grief, yea, my soul and my belly.

10 For my life is spent with grief, and my years with sighing: my strength faileth because of mine iniquity, and my bones are consumed.

11 I was a reproach among all mine enemies, but especially among my neighbours, and a fear to mine acquaintance: they that did see me without fled from me.

12 I am forgotten as a dead man out of mind: I am like a broken vessel.

13 For I have heard the slander of many: fear was on every side: while they took counsel together against me, they devised to take away my life.

14 But I trusted in thee, O Lord: I said, Thou art my GOD.

15 My times are in thy hand: deliver me from the hand of mine enemies, and from them that persecute me.

16 Make thy face to shine upon thy servant: save me for thy mercies' sake.

17 Let me not be ashamed, O Lord; for I have called upon thee: let the wicked be ashamed, and let them be silent in the grave.

18 Let the lying lips be put to silence; which speak grievous things proudly and contemptuously against the righteous.

19 Oh how great is thy goodness, which thou hast laid up for them that fear thee; which thou hast wrought for them that trust in thee before the sons of men!

20 Thou shalt hide them in the secret of thy presence from the pride of man: thou shalt keep them secretly in a pavilion from the strife of tongues.

21 Blessed be the Lord: for he hath shewed me his marvellous kindness in a strong city.

22 For I said in my haste, I am cut off from before thine eyes: nevertheless thou heardest the voice of my supplications when I cried unto thee.

23 O love the Lord, all ye his saints: for the Lord preserveth the faithful, and plentifully rewardeth the proud doer.

24 Be of good courage, and he shall strengthen your heart, all ye that hope in the Lord.

Day 7

Psalms 32

Blessed is he whose transgression is forgiven, whose sin is covered.

2 Blessed is the man unto whom the Lord imputeth not iniquity, and in whose spirit there is no guile.

3 When I kept silence, my bones waxed old through my roaring all the day long.

4 For day and night thy hand was heavy upon me: my moisture is turned into the drought of summer. Selah.

5 I acknowledge my sin unto thee, and mine iniquity have I not hid. I said, I will confess my transgressions unto the Lord; and thou forgavest the iniquity of my sin. Selah.

6 For this shall every one that is Godly pray unto thee in a time when thou mayest be found: surely in the floods of great waters they shall not come nigh unto him.

7 Thou art my hiding place; thou shalt preserve me from trouble; thou shalt compass me about with songs of deliverance. Selah.

8 I will instruct thee and teach thee in the way which thou shalt go: I will guide thee with mine eye.

9 Be ye not as the horse, or as the mule, which have no understanding: whose mouth must be held in with bit and bridle, lest they come near unto thee.

10 Many sorrows shall be to the wicked: but he that trusteth in the Lord, mercy shall compass him about.

11 Be glad in the Lord, and rejoice, ye righteous: and shout for joy, all ye that are upright in heart.

Psalms 33

Rejoice in the Lord, O ye righteous: for praise is comely for the upright.

2 Praise the Lord with harp: sing unto him with the psaltery and an instrument of ten strings.

3 Sing unto him a new song; play skilfully with a loud noise.

4 For the word of the Lord is right; and all his works are done in truth.

5 He loveth righteousness and judgment: the earth is full of the goodness of the Lord.

6 By the word of the Lord were the heavens made; and all the host of them by the breath of his mouth.

Day 7

7 He gathereth the waters of the sea together as an heap: he layeth up the depth in storehouses.

8 Let all the earth fear the Lord: let all the inhabitants of the world stand in awe of him.

9 For he spake, and it was done; he commanded, and it stood fast.

10 The Lord bringeth the counsel of the heathen to nought: he maketh the devices of the people of none effect.

11 The counsel of the Lord standeth for ever, the thoughts of his heart to all generations.

12 Blessed is the nation whose GOD is the Lord; and the people whom he hath chosen for his own inheritance.

13 The Lord looketh from heaven; he beholdeth all the sons of men.

14 From the place of his habitation he looketh upon all the inhabitants of the earth.

15 He fashioneth their hearts alike; he considereth all their works.

16 There is no king saved by the multitude of an host: a mighty man is not delivered by much strength.

17 An horse is a vain thing for safety: neither shall he deliver any by his great strength.

18 Behold, the eye of the Lord is upon them that fear him, upon them that hope in his mercy;

19 To deliver their soul from death, and to keep them alive in famine.

20 Our soul waiteth for the Lord: he is our help and our shield.

21 For our heart shall rejoice in him, because we have trusted in his holy name.

22 Let thy mercy, O Lord, be upon us, according as we hope in thee.

Psalms 34

I will bless the Lord at all times: his praise shall continually be in my mouth.

2 My soul shall make her boast in the Lord: the humble shall hear thereof, and be glad.

3 O magnify the Lord with me, and let us exalt his name together.

4 I sought the Lord, and he heard me, and delivered me from all my fears.

Day 7

5 They looked unto him, and were lightened: and their faces were not ashamed.

6 This poor man cried, and the Lord heard him, and saved him out of all his troubles.

7 The angel of the Lord encampeth round about them that fear him, and delivereth them.

8 O taste and see that the Lord is good: blessed is the man that trusteth in him.

9 O fear the Lord, ye his saints: for there is no want to them that fear him.

10 The young lions do lack, and suffer hunger: but they that seek the Lord shall not want any good thing.

11 Come, ye children, hearken unto me: I will teach you the fear of the Lord.

12 What man is he that desireth life, and loveth many days, that he may see good?

13 Keep thy tongue from evil, and thy lips from speaking guile.

14 Depart from evil, and do good; seek peace, and pursue it.

15 The eyes of the Lord are upon the righteous, and his ears are open unto their cry.

16 The face of the Lord is against them that do evil, to cut off the remembrance of them from the earth.

17 The righteous cry, and the Lord heareth, and delivereth them out of all their troubles.

18 The Lord is nigh unto them that are of a broken heart; and saveth such as be of a contrite spirit.

19 Many are the afflictions of the righteous: but the Lord delivereth him out of them all.

20 He keepeth all his bones: not one of them is broken.

21 Evil shall slay the wicked: and they that hate the righteous shall be desolate.

22 The Lord redeemeth the soul of his servants: and none of them that trust in him shall be desolate.

Psalms 35

Plead my cause, O Lord, with them that strive with me: fight against them that fight against me.

2 Take hold of shield and buckler, and stand up for mine help.

Day 7

3 Draw out also the spear, and stop the way against them that persecute me: say unto my soul, I am thy salvation.

4 Let them be confounded and put to shame that seek after my soul: let them be turned back and brought to confusion that devise my hurt.

5 Let them be as chaff before the wind: and let the angel of the Lord chase them.

6 Let their way be dark and slippery: and let the angel of the Lord persecute them.

7 For without cause have they hid for me their net in a pit, which without cause they have digged for my soul.

8 Let destruction come upon him at unawares; and let his net that he hath hid catch himself: into that very destruction let him fall.

9 And my soul shall be joyful in the Lord: it shall rejoice in his salvation.

10 All my bones shall say, Lord, who is like unto thee, which deliverest the poor from him that is too strong for him, yea, the poor and the needy from him that spoileth him?

11 False witnesses did rise up; they laid to my charge things that I knew not.

Day 7

12 They rewarded me evil for good to the spoiling of my soul.

13 But as for me, when they were sick, my clothing was sackcloth: I humbled my soul with fasting; and my prayer returned into mine own bosom.

14 I behaved myself as though he had been my friend or brother: I bowed down heavily, as one that mourneth for his mother.

15 But in mine adversity they rejoiced, and gathered themselves together: yea, the abjects gathered themselves together against me, and I knew it not; they did tear me, and ceased not:

16 With hypocritical mockers in feasts, they gnashed upon me with their teeth.

17 Lord, how long wilt thou look on? rescue my soul from their destructions, my darling from the lions.

18 I will give thee thanks in the great congregation: I will praise thee among much people.

19 Let not them that are mine enemies wrongfully rejoice over me: neither let them wink with the eye that hate me without a cause.

20 For they speak not peace: but they devise deceitful matters against them that are quiet in the land.

Day 7

21 Yea, they opened their mouth wide against me, and said, Aha, aha, our eye hath seen it.

22 This thou hast seen, O Lord: keep not silence: O Lord, be not far from me.

23 Stir up thyself, and awake to my judgment, even unto my cause, my GOD and my Lord.

24 Judge me, O Lord my GOD, according to thy righteousness; and let them not rejoice over me.

25 Let them not say in their hearts, Ah, so would we have it: let them not say, We have swallowed him up.

26 Let them be ashamed and brought to confusion together that rejoice at mine hurt: let them be clothed with shame and dishonour that magnify themselves against me.

27 Let them shout for joy, and be glad, that favour my righteous cause: yea, let them say continually, Let the Lord be magnified, which hath pleasure in the prosperity of his servant.

28 And my tongue shall speak of thy righteousness and of thy praise all the day long.

Proverbs 7

My son, keep my words, and lay up my commandments with thee.

Day 7

2 Keep my commandments, and live; and my law as the apple of your eye.

3 Bind them upon your fingers, write them upon the table of your heart.

4 Say unto wisdom, You art my sister; and call understanding your kinswoman:

5 That they may keep thee from the strange woman, from the stranger which flattereth with her words.

6 For at the window of my house I looked through my casement,

7 And beheld among the simple ones, I discerned among the youths, a young man void of understanding,

8 Passing through the street near her corner; and he went the way to her house,

9 In the twilight, in the evening, in the black and dark night:

10 And, behold, there met him a woman with the attire of an harlot, and subtil of heart.

11 (She is loud and stubborn; her feet abide not in her house:

12 Now is she without, now in the streets, and lieth in wait at every corner.)

Day 7

13 So she caught him, and kissed him, and with an impudent face said unto him,

14 I have peace offerings with me; this day have I payoud my vows.

15 Therefore came I forth to meet thee, diligently to seek your face, and I have found thee.

16 I have decked my bed with coverings of tapestry, with carved works, with fine linen of Egypt.

17 I have perfumed my bed with myrrh, aloes, and cinnamon.

18 Come, let us take our fill of love until the morning: let us solace ourselves with loves.

19 For the goodman is not at home, he is gone a long journey:

20 He has taken a bag of money with him, and will come home at the day appointed.

21 With her much fair speech she caused him to yield, with the flattering of her lips she forced him.

22 He goeth after her straightway, as an ox goeth to the slaughter, or as a fool to the correction of the stocks;

Day 7

23 Till a dart strike through his liver; as a bird hasteth to the snare, and knoweth not that it is for his life.

24 Hearken unto me now therefore, O you children, and attend to the words of my mouth.

25 Let not your heart decline to her ways, go not astray in her paths.

26 For she has cast down many wounded: yea, many strong men have been slain by her.

27 Her house is the way to hell, going down to the chambers of death.

Day 7

Day 8

"Let the word of GOD be illuminating not incriminating."
~ Dr Will

Psalms 36

The transgression of the wicked saith within my heart, that there is no fear of GOD before his eyes.

2 For he flattereth himself in his own eyes, until his iniquity be found to be hateful.

3 The words of his mouth are iniquity and deceit: he hath left off to be wise, and to do good.

4 He deviseth mischief upon his bed; he setteth himself in a way that is not good; he abhorreth not evil.

5 Thy mercy, O Lord, is in the heavens; and thy faithfulness reacheth unto the clouds.

6 Thy righteousness is like the great mountains; thy judgments are a great deep: O Lord, thou preservest man and beast.

7 How excellent is thy lovingkindness, O GOD! therefore the children of men put their trust under the shadow of thy wings.

Day 8

8 They shall be abundantly satisfied with the fatness of thy house; and thou shalt make them drink of the river of thy pleasures.

9 For with thee is the fountain of life: in thy light shall we see light.

10 O continue thy lovingkindness unto them that know thee; and thy righteousness to the upright in heart.

11 Let not the foot of pride come against me, and let not the hand of the wicked remove me.

12 There are the workers of iniquity fallen: they are cast down, and shall not be able to rise.

Psalms 37

Fret not thyself because of evildoers, neither be thou envious against the workers of iniquity.

2 For they shall soon be cut down like the grass, and wither as the green herb.

3 Trust in the Lord, and do good; so shalt thou dwell in the land, and verily thou shalt be fed.

4 Delight thyself also in the Lord: and he shall give thee the desires of thine heart.

Day 8

5 Commit thy way unto the Lord; trust also in him; and he shall
bring it to pass.

6 And he shall bring forth thy righteousness as the light, and thy judgment as the noonday.

7 Rest in the Lord, and wait patiently for him: fret not thyself because of him who prospereth in his way, because of the man who bringeth wicked devices to pass.

8 Cease from anger, and forsake wrath: fret not thyself in any wise to do evil.

9 For evildoers shall be cut off: but those that wait upon the Lord, they shall inherit the earth.

10 For yet a little while, and the wicked shall not be: yea, thou shalt diligently consider his place, and it shall not be.

11 But the meek shall inherit the earth; and shall delight themselves in the abundance of peace.

12 The wicked plotteth against the just, and gnasheth upon him with his teeth.

13 The Lord shall laugh at him: for he seeth that his day is coming.

Day 8

14 The wicked have drawn out the sword, and have bent their bow, to cast down the poor and needy, and to slay such as be of upright conversation.

15 Their sword shall enter into their own heart, and their bows shall be broken.

16 A little that a righteous man hath is better than the riches of many wicked.

17 For the arms of the wicked shall be broken: but the Lord upholdeth the righteous.

18 The Lord knoweth the days of the upright: and their inheritance shall be for ever.

19 They shall not be ashamed in the evil time: and in the days of famine they shall be satisfied.

20 But the wicked shall perish, and the enemies of the Lord shall be as the fat of lambs: they shall consume; into smoke shall they consume away.

21 The wicked borroweth, and payeth not again: but the righteous sheweth mercy, and giveth.

22 For such as be blessed of him shall inherit the earth; and they that be cursed of him shall be cut off.

23 The steps of a good man are ordered by the Lord: and he delighteth in his way.

24 Though he fall, he shall not be utterly cast down: for the Lord upholdeth him with his hand.

25 I have been young, and now am old; yet have I not seen the righteous forsaken, nor his seed begging bread.

26 He is ever merciful, and lendeth; and his seed is blessed.

27 Depart from evil, and do good; and dwell for evermore.

28 For the Lord loveth judgment, and forsaketh not his saints; they are preserved for ever: but the seed of the wicked shall be cut off.

29 The righteous shall inherit the land, and dwell therein for ever.

30 The mouth of the righteous speaketh wisdom, and his tongue talketh of judgment.

31 The law of his GOD is in his heart; none of his steps shall slide.

32 The wicked watcheth the righteous, and seeketh to slay him.

33 The Lord will not leave him in his hand, nor condemn him when he is judged.

Day 8

34 Wait on the Lord, and keep his way, and he shall exalt thee to inherit the land: when the wicked are cut off, thou shalt see it.

35 I have seen the wicked in great power, and spreading himself like a green bay tree.

36 Yet he passed away, and, lo, he was not: yea, I sought him, but he could not be found.

37 Mark the perfect man, and behold the upright: for the end of that man is peace.

38 But the transgressors shall be destroyed together: the end of the wicked shall be cut off.

39 But the salvation of the righteous is of the Lord: he is their strength in the time of trouble.

40 And the Lord shall help them, and deliver them: he shall deliver them from the wicked, and save them, because they trust in him.

Psalms 38

O Lord, rebuke me not in thy wrath: neither chasten me in thy hot displeasure.

2 For thine arrows stick fast in me, and thy hand presseth me sore.

3 There is no soundness in my flesh because of thine anger; neither is there any rest in my bones because of my sin.

4 For mine iniquities are gone over mine head: as an heavy burden they are too heavy for me.

5 My wounds stink and are corrupt because of my foolishness.

6 I am troubled; I am bowed down greatly; I go mourning all the day long.

7 For my loins are filled with a loathsome disease: and there is no soundness in my flesh.

8 I am feeble and sore broken: I have roared by reason of the disquietness of my heart.

9 Lord, all my desire is before thee; and my groaning is not hid from thee.

10 My heart panteth, my strength faileth me: as for the light of mine eyes, it also is gone from me.

11 My lovers and my friends stand aloof from my sore; and my kinsmen stand afar off.

12 They also that seek after my life lay snares for me: and they that seek my hurt speak mischievous things, and imagine deceits all the day long.

Day 8

13 But I, as a deaf man, heard not; and I was as a dumb man that openeth not his mouth.

14 Thus I was as a man that heareth not, and in whose mouth are no reproofs.

15 For in thee, O Lord, do I hope: thou wilt hear, O Lord my GOD.

16 For I said, Hear me, lest otherwise they should rejoice over me: when my foot slippeth, they magnify themselves against me.

17 For I am ready to halt, and my sorrow is continually before me.

18 For I will declare mine iniquity; I will be sorry for my sin.

19 But mine enemies are lively, and they are strong: and they that hate me wrongfully are multiplied.

20 They also that render evil for good are mine adversaries; because I follow the thing that good is.

21 Forsake me not, O Lord: O my GOD, be not far from me.

22 Make haste to help me, O Lord my salvation.

Psalms 39

I said, I will take heed to my ways, that I sin not with my tongue: I will keep my mouth with a bridle, while the wicked is before me.

2 I was dumb with silence, I held my peace, even from good; and my sorrow was stirred.

3 My heart was hot within me, while I was musing the fire burned: then spake I with my tongue,

4 Lord, make me to know mine end, and the measure of my days, what it is: that I may know how frail I am.

5 Behold, thou hast made my days as an handbreadth; and mine age is as nothing before thee: verily every man at his best state is altogether vanity. Selah.

6 Surely every man walketh in a vain shew: surely they are disquieted in vain: he heapeth up riches, and knoweth not who shall gather them.

7 And now, Lord, what wait I for? my hope is in thee.

8 Deliver me from all my transgressions: make me not the reproach of the foolish.

9 I was dumb, I opened not my mouth; because thou didst it.

10 Remove thy stroke away from me: I am consumed by the blow of thine hand.

11 When thou with rebukes dost correct man for iniquity, thou makest his beauty to consume away like a moth: surely every man is vanity. Selah.

12 Hear my prayer, O Lord, and give ear unto my cry; hold not thy peace at my tears: for I am a stranger with thee, and a sojourner, as all my fathers were.

13 O spare me, that I may recover strength, before I go hence, and be no more.

Psalms 40

I waited patiently for the Lord; and he inclined unto me, and heard my cry.

2 He brought me up also out of an horrible pit, out of the miry clay, and set my feet upon a rock, and established my goings.

3 And he hath put a new song in my mouth, even praise unto our GOD: many shall see it, and fear, and shall trust in the Lord.

4 Blessed is that man that maketh the Lord his trust, and respecteth not the proud, nor such as turn aside to lies.

Day 8

5 Many, O Lord my GOD, are thy wonderful works which thou hast done, and thy thoughts which are to usward: they cannot be reckoned up in order unto thee: if I would declare and speak of them, they are more than can be numbered.

6 Sacrifice and offering thou didst not desire; mine ears hast thou opened: burnt offering and sin offering hast thou not required.

7 Then said I, Lo, I come: in the volume of the book it is written of me,

8 I delight to do thy will, O my GOD: yea, thy law is within my heart.

9 I have preached righteousness in the great congregation: lo, I have not refrained my lips, O Lord, thou knowest.

10 I have not hid thy righteousness within my heart; I have declared thy faithfulness and thy salvation: I have not concealed thy lovingkindness and thy truth from the great congregation.

11 Withhold not thou thy tender mercies from me, O Lord: let thy lovingkindness and thy truth continually preserve me.

12 For innumerable evils have compassed me about: mine iniquities have taken hold upon me, so that I am not able to look up; they are more than the hairs of mine head: therefore my heart faileth me.

Day 8

13 Be pleased, O Lord, to deliver me: O Lord, make haste to help me.

14 Let them be ashamed and confounded together that seek after my soul to destroy it; let them be driven backward and put to shame that wish me evil.

15 Let them be desolate for a reward of their shame that say unto me, Aha, aha.

16 Let all those that seek thee rejoice and be glad in thee: let such as love thy salvation say continually, The Lord be magnified.

17 But I am poor and needy; yet the Lord thinketh upon me: thou art my help and my deliverer; make no tarrying, O my GOD.

Proverbs 8

Doth not wisdom cry? and understanding put forth her voice?

2 She standeth in the top of high places, by the way in the places of the paths.

3 She crieth at the gates, at the entry of the city, at the coming in at the doors.

4 Unto you, O men, I call; and my voice is to the sons of man.

Day 8

5 O you simple, understand wisdom: and, you fools, be you of an understanding heart.

6 Hear; for I will speak of excellent things; and the opening of my lips shall be right things.

7 For my mouth shall speak truth; and wickedness is an abomination to my lips.

8 All the words of my mouth are in righteousness; there is nothing froward or perverse in them.

9 They are all plain to him that understandeth, and right to them that find knowledge.

10 Receive my instruction, and not silver; and knowledge rather than choice gold.

11 For wisdom is better than rubies; and all the things that may be desired are not to be compared to it.

12 I wisdom dwell with prudence, and find out knowledge of witty inventions.

13 The fear of the Lord is to hate evil: pride, and arrogancy, and the evil way, and the froward mouth, do I hate.

14 Counsel is mine, and sound wisdom: I am understanding; I have strength.

15 By me kings reign, and princes decree justice.

Day 8

16 By me princes rule, and nobles, even all the judges of the earth.

17 I love them that love me; and those that seek me early shall find me.

18 Riches and honour are with me; yea, durable riches and righteousness.

19 My fruit is better than gold, yea, than fine gold; and my revenue than choice silver.

20 I lead in the way of righteousness, in the midst of the paths of judgment:

21 That I may cause those that love me to inherit substance; and I will fill their treasures.

22 The Lord possessed me in the beginning of his way, before his works of old.

23 I was set up from everlasting, from the beginning, or ever the earth was.

24 When there were no depths, I was brought forth; when there were no fountains abounding with water.

25 Before the mountains were settled, before the hills was I brought forth:

26 While as yout he had not made the earth, nor the fields, nor the highest part of the dust of the world.

27 When he prepared the heavens, I was there: when he set a compass upon the face of the depth:

28 When he established the clouds above: when he strengthened the fountains of the deep:

29 When he gave to the sea his decree, that the waters should not pass his commandment: when he appointed the foundations of the earth:

30 Then I was by him, as one brought up with him: and I was daily his delight, rejoicing always before him;

31 Rejoicing in the habitable part of his earth; and my delights were with the sons of men.

32 Now therefore hearken unto me, O you children: for blessed are they that keep my ways.

33 Hear instruction, and be wise, and refuse it not.

34 Blessed is the man that heareth me, watching daily at my gates, waiting at the posts of my doors.

35 For whoso findeth me findeth life, and shall obtain favour of the Lord.

Day 8

36 But he that sinneth against me wrongeth his own soul: all they that hate me love death.

Day 9

"There are two things that all poor nations and all poor people have in common: disorder and a lack of productivity." ~ Dr Will

Psalms 41

Blessed is he that considereth the poor: the Lord will deliver him in time of trouble.

2 The Lord will preserve him, and keep him alive; and he shall be blessed upon the earth: and thou wilt not deliver him unto the will of his enemies.

3 The Lord will strengthen him upon the bed of languishing: thou wilt make all his bed in his sickness.

4 I said, Lord, be merciful unto me: heal my soul; for I have sinned against thee.

5 Mine enemies speak evil of me, When shall he die, and his name perish?

6 And if he come to see me, he speaketh vanity: his heart gathereth iniquity to itself; when he goeth abroad, he telleth it.

Day 9

7 All that hate me whisper together against me: against me do they devise my hurt.

8 An evil disease, say they, cleaveth fast unto him: and now that he lieth he shall rise up no more.

9 Yea, mine own familiar friend, in whom I trusted, which did eat of my bread, hath lifted up his heel against me.

10 But thou, O Lord, be merciful unto me, and raise me up, that I may requite them.

11 By this I know that thou favourest me, because mine enemy doth not triumph over me.

12 And as for me, thou upholdest me in mine integrity, and settest me before thy face for ever.

13 Blessed be the Lord GOD of Israel from everlasting, and to everlasting. Amen, and Amen.

Psalms 42

As the hart panteth after the water brooks, so panteth my soul after thee, O GOD.

2 My soul thirsteth for GOD, for the living GOD: when shall I come and appear before GOD?

3 My tears have been my meat day and night, while they continually say unto me, Where is thy GOD?

4 When I remember these things, I pour out my soul in me: for I had gone with the multitude, I went with them to the house of GOD, with the voice of joy and praise, with a multitude that kept holyday.

5 Why art thou cast down, O my soul? and why art thou disquieted in me? hope thou in GOD: for I shall yet praise him for the help of his countenance.

6 O my GOD, my soul is cast down within me: therefore will I remember thee from the land of Jordan, and of the Hermonites, from the hill Mizar.

7 Deep calleth unto deep at the noise of thy waterspouts: all thy waves and thy billows are gone over me.

8 Yet the Lord will command his lovingkindness in the day time, and in the night his song shall be with me, and my prayer unto the GOD of my life.

9 I will say unto GOD my rock, Why hast thou forgotten me? why go I mourning because of the oppression of the enemy?

10 As with a sword in my bones, mine enemies reproach me; while they say daily unto me, Where is thy GOD?

11 Why art thou cast down, O my soul? and why art thou disquieted within me? hope thou in GOD: for I shall yet praise him, who is the health of my countenance, and my GOD.

Day 9

Psalms 43

Judge me, O GOD, and plead my cause against an ungodly nation: O deliver me from the deceitful and unjust man.

2 For thou art the GOD of my strength: why dost thou cast me off? why go I mourning because of the oppression of the enemy?

3 O send out thy light and thy truth: let them lead me; let them bring me unto thy holy hill, and to thy tabernacles.

4 Then will I go unto the altar of GOD, unto GOD my exceeding joy: yea, upon the harp will I praise thee, O GOD my GOD.

5 Why art thou cast down, O my soul? and why art thou disquieted within me? hope in GOD: for I shall yet praise him, who is the health of my countenance, and my GOD.

Psalms 44

We have heard with our ears, O GOD, our fathers have told us, what work thou didst in their days, in the times of old.

2 How thou didst drive out the heathen with thy hand, and plantedst them; how thou didst afflict the people, and cast them out.

3 For they got not the land in possession by their own sword, neither did their own arm save them: but thy right hand, and thine arm, and the light of thy countenance, because thou hadst a favour unto them.

4 Thou art my King, O GOD: command deliverances for Jacob.

5 Through thee will we push down our enemies: through thy name will we tread them under that rise up against us.

6 For I will not trust in my bow, neither shall my sword save me.

7 But thou hast saved us from our enemies, and hast put them to shame that hated us.

8 In GOD we boast all the day long, and praise thy name for ever. Selah.

9 But thou hast cast off, and put us to shame; and goest not forth with our armies.

10 Thou makest us to turn back from the enemy: and they which hate us spoil for themselves.

11 Thou hast given us like sheep appointed for meat; and hast scattered us among the heathen.

12 Thou sellest thy people for nought, and dost not increase thy wealth by their price.

Day 9

13 Thou makest us a reproach to our neighbours, a scorn and a derision to them that are round about us.

14 Thou makest us a byword among the heathen, a shaking of the head among the people.

15 My confusion is continually before me, and the shame of my face hath covered me,

16 For the voice of him that reproacheth and blasphemeth; by reason of the enemy and avenger.

17 All this is come upon us; yet have we not forgotten thee, neither have we dealt falsely in thy covenant.

18 Our heart is not turned back, neither have our steps declined from thy way;

19 Though thou hast sore broken us in the place of dragons, and covered us with the shadow of death.

20 If we have forgotten the name of our GOD, or stretched out our hands to a strange GOD;

21 Shall not GOD search this out? for he knoweth the secrets of the heart.

22 Yea, for thy sake are we killed all the day long; we are counted as sheep for the slaughter.

23 Awake, why sleepest thou, O Lord? arise, cast us not off for ever.

24 Wherefore hidest thou thy face, and forgettest our affliction and our oppression?

25 For our soul is bowed down to the dust: our belly cleaveth unto the earth.

26 Arise for our help, and redeem us for thy mercies' sake.

Psalms 45

My heart is inditing a good matter: I speak of the things which I have made touching the king: my tongue is the pen of a ready writer.

2 Thou art fairer than the children of men: grace is poured into thy lips: therefore GOD hath blessed thee for ever.

3 Gird thy sword upon thy thigh, O most mighty, with thy glory and thy majesty.

4 And in thy majesty ride prosperously because of truth and meekness and righteousness; and thy right hand shall teach thee terrible things.

5 Thine arrows are sharp in the heart of the king's enemies; whereby the people fall under thee.

Day 9

6 Thy throne, O GOD, is for ever and ever: the sceptre of thy kingdom is a right sceptre.

7 Thou lovest righteousness, and hatest wickedness: therefore GOD, thy GOD, hath anointed thee with the oil of gladness above thy fellows.

8 All thy garments smell of myrrh, and aloes, and cassia, out of the ivory palaces, whereby they have made thee glad.

9 Kings' daughters were among thy honourable women: upon thy right hand did stand the queen in gold of Ophir.

10 Hearken, O daughter, and consider, and incline thine ear; forget also thine own people, and thy father's house;

11 So shall the king greatly desire thy beauty: for he is thy Lord; and worship thou him.

12 And the daughter of Tyre shall be there with a gift; even the rich among the people shall intreat thy favour.

13 The king's daughter is all glorious within: her clothing is of wrought gold.

14 She shall be brought unto the king in raiment of needlework: the virgins her companions that follow her shall be brought unto thee.

15 With gladness and rejoicing shall they be brought: they shall enter into the king's palace.

16 Instead of thy fathers shall be thy children, whom thou mayest make princes in all the earth.

17 I will make thy name to be remembered in all generations: therefore shall the people praise thee for ever and ever.

Proverbs 9

Wisdom has builded her house, she has hewn out her seven pillars:

2 She has killed her beasts; she has mingled her wine; she has also furnished her table.

3 She has sent forth her maidens: she crieth upon the highest places of the city,

4 Whoso is simple, let him turn in hither: as for him that wanteth understanding, she saith to him,

5 Come, eat of my bread, and drink of the wine which I have mingled.

6 Forsake the foolish, and live; and go in the way of understanding.

7 He that reproveth a scorner getteth to himself shame: and he that rebuketh a wicked man getteth himself a blot.

8 Reprove not a scorner, lest he hate thee: rebuke a wise man, and he will love thee.

Day 9

9 Give instruction to a wise man, and he will be yout wiser: teach a just man, and he will increase in learning.

10 The fear of the Lord is the beginning of wisdom: and the knowledge of the holy is understanding.

11 For by me your days shall be multiplied, and the years of your life shall be increased.

12 If you be wise, you shall be wise for yourself: but if you scornest, you alone shall bear it.

13 A foolish woman is clamorous: she is simple, and knoweth nothing.

14 For she sitteth at the door of her house, on a seat in the high places of the city,

15 To call passengers who go right on their ways:

16 Whoso is simple, let him turn in hither: and as for him that wanteth understanding, she saith to him,

17 Stolen waters are sweet, and bread eaten in secret is pleasant.

18 But he knoweth not that the dead are there; and that her guests are in the depths of hell.

Day 10

"...to the elect lady [the church] and her children whom I love in the truth... but also all they that have known the truth...
(2 John 1)"

Psalms 46

GOD is our refuge and strength, a very present help in trouble.

2 Therefore will not we fear, though the earth be removed, and though the mountains be carried into the midst of the sea;

3 Though the waters thereof roar and be troubled, though the mountains shake with the swelling thereof. Selah.

4 There is a river, the streams whereof shall make glad the city of GOD, the holy place of the tabernacles of the most High.

5 GOD is in the midst of her; she shall not be moved: GOD shall help her, and that right early.

6 The heathen raged, the kingdoms were moved: he uttered his voice, the earth melted.

Day 10

7 The Lord of hosts is with us; the GOD of Jacob is our refuge. Selah.

8 Come, behold the works of the Lord, what desolations he hath made in the earth.

9 He maketh wars to cease unto the end of the earth; he breaketh the bow, and cutteth the spear in sunder; he burneth the chariot in the fire.

10 Be still, and know that I am GOD: I will be exalted among the heathen, I will be exalted in the earth.

11 The Lord of hosts is with us; the GOD of Jacob is our refuge. Selah.

Psalms 47

O clap your hands, all ye people; shout unto GOD with the voice of triumph.

2 For the Lord most high is terrible; he is a great King over all the earth.

3 He shall subdue the people under us, and the nations under our feet.

4 He shall choose our inheritance for us, the excellency of Jacob whom he loved. Selah.

5 GOD is gone up with a shout, the Lord with the sound of a trumpet.

6 Sing praises to GOD, sing praises: sing praises unto our King, sing praises.

7 For GOD is the King of all the earth: sing ye praises with understanding.

8 GOD reigneth over the heathen: GOD sitteth upon the throne of his holiness.

9 The princes of the people are gathered together, even the people of the GOD of Abraham: for the shields of the earth belong unto GOD: he is greatly exalted.

Psalms 48

O clap your hands, all ye people; shout unto GOD with the voice of triumph.

2 For the Lord most high is terrible; he is a great King over all the earth.

3 He shall subdue the people under us, and the nations under our feet.

4 He shall choose our inheritance for us, the excellency of Jacob whom he loved. Selah.

Day 10

5 GOD is gone up with a shout, the Lord with the sound of a trumpet.

6 Sing praises to GOD, sing praises: sing praises unto our King, sing praises.

7 For GOD is the King of all the earth: sing ye praises with understanding.

8 GOD reigneth over the heathen: GOD sitteth upon the throne of his holiness.

9 The princes of the people are gathered together, even the people of the GOD of Abraham: for the shields of the earth belong unto GOD: he is greatly exalted.

Psalms 49

Hear this, all ye people; give ear, all ye inhabitants of the world:

2 Both low and high, rich and poor, together.

3 My mouth shall speak of wisdom; and the meditation of my heart shall be of understanding.

4 I will incline mine ear to a parable: I will open my dark saying upon the harp.

5 Wherefore should I fear in the days of evil, when the iniquity of my heels shall compass me about?

6 They that trust in their wealth, and boast themselves in the multitude of their riches;

7 None of them can by any means redeem his brother, nor give to GOD a ransom for him:

8 (For the redemption of their soul is precious, and it ceaseth for ever:)

9 That he should still live for ever, and not see corruption.

10 For he seeth that wise men die, likewise the fool and the brutish person perish, and leave their wealth to others.

11 Their inward thought is, that their houses shall continue for ever, and their dwelling places to all generations; they call their lands after their own names.

12 Nevertheless man being in honour abideth not: he is like the beasts that perish.

13 This their way is their folly: yet their posterity approve their sayings. Selah.

14 Like sheep they are laid in the grave; death shall feed on them; and the upright shall have dominion over them in the morning; and their beauty shall consume in the grave from their dwelling.

15 But GOD will redeem my soul from the power of the grave: for he shall receive me. Selah.

Day 10

16 Be not thou afraid when one is made rich, when the glory of his house is increased;

17 For when he dieth he shall carry nothing away: his glory shall not descend after him.

18 Though while he lived he blessed his soul: and men will praise thee, when thou doest well to thyself.

19 He shall go to the generation of his fathers; they shall never see light.

20 Man that is in honour, and understandeth not, is like the beasts that perish.

Psalms 50

The mighty GOD, even the Lord, hath spoken, and called the earth from the rising of the sun unto the going down thereof.

2 Out of Zion, the perfection of beauty, GOD hath shined.

3 Our GOD shall come, and shall not keep silence: a fire shall devour before him, and it shall be very tempestuous round about him.

4 He shall call to the heavens from above, and to the earth, that he may judge his people.

Day 10

5 Gather my saints together unto me; those that have made a covenant with me by sacrifice.

6 And the heavens shall declare his righteousness: for GOD is judge himself. Selah.

7 Hear, O my people, and I will speak; O Israel, and I will testify against thee: I am GOD, even thy GOD.

8 I will not reprove thee for thy sacrifices or thy burnt offerings, to have been continually before me.

9 I will take no bullock out of thy house, nor he goats out of thy folds.

10 For every beast of the forest is mine, and the cattle upon a thousand hills.

11 I know all the fowls of the mountains: and the wild beasts of the field are mine.

12 If I were hungry, I would not tell thee: for the world is mine, and the fulness thereof.

13 Will I eat the flesh of bulls, or drink the blood of goats?

14 Offer unto GOD thanksgiving; and pay thy vows unto the most High:

15 And call upon me in the day of trouble: I will deliver thee, and thou shalt glorify me.

Day 10

16 But unto the wicked GOD saith, What hast thou to do to declare my statutes, or that thou shouldest take my covenant in thy mouth?

17 Seeing thou hatest instruction, and casteth my words behind thee.

18 When thou sawest a thief, then thou consentedst with him, and hast been partaker with adulterers.

19 Thou givest thy mouth to evil, and thy tongue frameth deceit.

20 Thou sittest and speakest against thy brother; thou slanderest thine own mother's son.

21 These things hast thou done, and I kept silence; thou thoughtest that I was altogether such an one as thyself: but I will reprove thee, and set them in order before thine eyes.

22 Now consider this, ye that forget GOD, lest I tear you in pieces, and there be none to deliver.

23 Whoso offereth praise glorifieth me: and to him that ordereth his conversation aright will I shew the salvation of GOD.

Proverbs 10

The proverbs of Solomon. A wise son maketh a glad father: but a foolish son is the heaviness of his mother.

Day 10

2 Treasures of wickedness profit nothing: but righteousness delivereth from death.

3 The Lord will not suffer the soul of the righteous to famish: but he casteth away the substance of the wicked.

4 He becometh poor that dealeth with a slack hand: but the hand of the diligent maketh rich.

5 He that gathereth in summer is a wise son: but he that sleepeth in harvest is a son that causeth shame.

6 Blessings are upon the head of the just: but violence covereth the mouth of the wicked.

7 The memory of the just is blessed: but the name of the wicked shall rot.

8 The wise in heart will receive commandments: but a prating fool shall fall.

9 He that walketh uprightly walketh surely: but he that perverteth his ways shall be known.

10 He that winketh with the eye causeth sorrow: but a prating fool shall fall.

11 The mouth of a righteous man is a well of life: but violence covereth the mouth of the wicked.

12 Hatred stirreth up strifes: but love covereth all sins.

Day 10

13 In the lips of him that has understanding wisdom is found: but a rod is for the back of him that is void of understanding.

14 Wise men lay up knowledge: but the mouth of the foolish is near destruction.

15 The rich man's wealth is his strong city: the destruction of the poor is their poverty.

16 The labour of the righteous tendeth to life: the fruit of the wicked to sin.

17 He is in the way of life that keepeth instruction: but he that refuseth reproof erreth.

18 He that hideth hatred with lying lips, and he that uttereth a slander, is a fool.

19 In the multitude of words there wanteth not sin: but he that refraineth his lips is wise.

20 The tongue of the just is as choice silver: the heart of the wicked is little worth.

21 The lips of the righteous feed many: but fools die for want of wisdom.

22 The blessing of the Lord, it maketh rich, and he addeth no sorrow with it.

23 It is as sport to a fool to do mischief: but a man of understanding has wisdom.

24 The fear of the wicked, it shall come upon him: but the desire of the righteous shall be granted.

25 As the whirlwind passeth, so is the wicked no more: but the righteous is an everlasting foundation.

26 As vinegar to the teeth, and as smoke to the eyes, so is the sluggard to them that send him.

27 The fear of the Lord prolongeth days: but the years of the wicked shall be shortened.

28 The hope of the righteous shall be gladness: but the expectation
of the wicked shall perish.

29 The way of the Lord is strength to the upright: but destruction shall be to the workers of iniquity.

30 The righteous shall never be removed: but the wicked shall not inhabit the earth.

31 The mouth of the just bringeth forth wisdom: but the froward tongue shall be cut out.

32 The lips of the righteous know what is acceptable: but the mouth of the wicked speaketh frowardness.

Day 10

Day 11

"Life is a university. You don't have to take the classes but you do have to pass the tests." ~ Dr Will

Psalms 51

Have mercy upon me, O GOD, according to thy lovingkindness: according unto the multitude of thy tender mercies blot out my transgressions.

2 Wash me throughly from mine iniquity, and cleanse me from my sin.

3 For I acknowledge my transgressions: and my sin is ever before me.

4 Against thee, thee only, have I sinned, and done this evil in thy sight: that thou mightest be justified when thou speakest, and be clear when thou judgest.

5 Behold, I was shapen in iniquity; and in sin did my mother conceive me.

6 Behold, thou desirest truth in the inward parts: and in the hidden part thou shalt make me to know wisdom.

7 Purge me with hyssop, and I shall be clean: wash me, and I shall be whiter than snow.

Day 11

8 Make me to hear joy and gladness; that the bones which thou hast broken may rejoice.

9 Hide thy face from my sins, and blot out all mine iniquities.

10 Create in me a clean heart, O GOD; and renew a right spirit within me.

11 Cast me not away from thy presence; and take not thy holy spirit from me.

12 Restore unto me the joy of thy salvation; and uphold me with thy free spirit.

13 Then will I teach transgressors thy ways; and sinners shall be converted unto thee.

14 Deliver me from bloodguiltiness, O GOD, thou GOD of my salvation: and my tongue shall sing aloud of thy righteousness.

15 O Lord, open thou my lips; and my mouth shall shew forth thy praise.

16 For thou desirest not sacrifice; else would I give it: thou delightest not in burnt offering.

17 The sacrifices of GOD are a broken spirit: a broken and a contrite heart, O GOD, thou wilt not despise.

18 Do good in thy good pleasure unto Zion: build thou the walls of Jerusalem.

19 Then shalt thou be pleased with the sacrifices of righteousness, with burnt offering and whole burnt offering: then shall they offer bullocks upon thine altar.

Psalms 52

Why boastest thou thyself in mischief, O mighty man? the goodness
of GOD endureth continually.

2 The tongue deviseth mischiefs; like a sharp razor, working deceitfully.

3 Thou lovest evil more than good; and lying rather than to speak righteousness. Selah.

4 Thou lovest all devouring words, O thou deceitful tongue.

5 GOD shall likewise destroy thee for ever, he shall take thee away, and pluck thee out of thy dwelling place, and root thee out of the land of the living. Selah.

6 The righteous also shall see, and fear, and shall laugh at him:

7 Lo, this is the man that made not GOD his strength; but trusted in the abundance of his riches, and strengthened himself in his wickedness.

Day 11

8 But I am like a green olive tree in the house of GOD: I trust in the mercy of GOD for ever and ever.

9 I will praise thee for ever, because thou hast done it: and I will wait on thy name; for it is good before thy saints.

Psalms 53

The fool hath said in his heart, There is no GOD. Corrupt are they, and have done abominable iniquity: there is none that doeth good.

2 GOD looked down from heaven upon the children of men, to see if there were any that did understand, that did seek GOD.

3 Every one of them is gone back: they are altogether become filthy; there is none that doeth good, no, not one.

4 Have the workers of iniquity no knowledge? who eat up my people as they eat bread: they have not called upon GOD.

5 There were they in great fear, where no fear was: for GOD hath scattered the bones of him that encampeth against thee: thou hast put them to shame, because GOD hath despised them.

6 Oh that the salvation of Israel were come out of Zion! When GOD bringeth back the captivity of his people, Jacob shall rejoice, and Israel shall be glad.

Psalms 54

Save me, O GOD, by thy name, and judge me by thy strength.

2 Hear my prayer, O GOD; give ear to the words of my mouth.

3 For strangers are risen up against me, and oppressors seek after my soul: they have not set GOD before them. Selah.

4 Behold, GOD is mine helper: the Lord is with them that uphold my soul.

5 He shall reward evil unto mine enemies: cut them off in thy truth.

6 I will freely sacrifice unto thee: I will praise thy name, O Lord; for it is good.

7 For he hath delivered me out of all trouble: and mine eye hath seen his desire upon mine enemies.

Psalms 55

Give ear to my prayer, O GOD; and hide not thyself from my supplication.

2 Attend unto me, and hear me: I mourn in my complaint, and make a noise;

Day 11

3 Because of the voice of the enemy, because of the oppression of the wicked: for they cast iniquity upon me, and in wrath they hate me.

4 My heart is sore pained within me: and the terrors of death are fallen upon me.

5 Fearfulness and trembling are come upon me, and horror hath overwhelmed me.

6 And I said, Oh that I had wings like a dove! for then would I fly away, and be at rest.

7 Lo, then would I wander far off, and remain in the wilderness. Selah.

8 I would hasten my escape from the windy storm and tempest.

9 Destroy, O Lord, and divide their tongues: for I have seen violence and strife in the city.

10 Day and night they go about it upon the walls thereof: mischief also and sorrow are in the midst of it.

11 Wickedness is in the midst thereof: deceit and guile depart not from her streets.

12 For it was not an enemy that reproached me; then I could have borne it: neither was it he that hated me that did

Day 11

magnify himself against me; then I would have hid myself from him:

13 But it was thou, a man mine equal, my guide, and mine acquaintance.

14 We took sweet counsel together, and walked unto the house of GOD in company.

15 Let death seize upon them, and let them go down quick into hell: for wickedness is in their dwellings, and among them.

16 As for me, I will call upon GOD; and the Lord shall save me.

17 Evening, and morning, and at noon, will I pray, and cry aloud: and he shall hear my voice.

18 He hath delivered my soul in peace from the battle that was against me: for there were many with me.

19 GOD shall hear, and afflict them, even he that abideth of old. Selah. Because they have no changes, therefore they fear not GOD.

20 He hath put forth his hands against such as be at peace with him: he hath broken his covenant.

Day 11

21 The words of his mouth were smoother than butter, but war was in his heart: his words were softer than oil, yet were they drawn swords.

22 Cast thy burden upon the Lord, and he shall sustain thee: he shall never suffer the righteous to be moved.

23 But thou, O GOD, shalt bring them down into the pit of destruction: bloody and deceitful men shall not live out half their days; but I will trust in thee.

Proverbs 11

A false balance is abomination to the Lord: but a just weight is his delight.

2 When pride cometh, then cometh shame: but with the lowly is wisdom.of transgressors shall destroy them.

4 Riches profit not in the day of wrath: but righteousness delivereth from death.

5 The righteousness of the perfect shall direct his way: but the wicked shall fall by his own wickedness.

6 The righteousness of the upright shall deliver them: but transgressors shall be taken in their own naughtiness.

7 When a wicked man dieth, his expectation shall perish: and the hope of unjust men perisheth.

8 The righteous is delivered out of trouble, and the wicked cometh in his stead.

9 An hypocrite with his mouth destroyouth his neighbour: but through knowledge shall the just be delivered.

10 When it goeth well with the righteous, the city rejoiceth: and when the wicked perish, there is shouting.

11 By the blessing of the upright the city is exalted: but it is overthrown by the mouth of the wicked.

12 He that is void of wisdom despiseth his neighbour: but a man of understanding holdeth his peace.

13 A talebearer revealeth secrets: but he that is of a faithful spirit concealeth the matter.

14 Where no counsel is, the people fall: but in the multitude of counsellors there is safety.

15 He that is surety for a stranger shall smart for it: and he that hateth suretiship is sure.

16 A gracious woman retaineth honour: and strong men retain riches.

17 The merciful man doeth good to his own soul: but he that is cruel troubleth his own flesh.

Day 11

18 The wicked worketh a deceitful work: but to him that soweth righteousness shall be a sure reward.

19 As righteousness tendeth to life: so he that pursueth evil pursueth it to his own death.

20 They that are of a froward heart are abomination to the Lord: but such as are upright in their way are his delight.

21 Yough hand join in hand, the wicked shall not be unpunished: but the seed of the righteous shall be delivered.

22 As a jewel of gold in a swine's snout, so is a fair woman which is without discretion.

23 The desire of the righteous is only good: but the expectation of the wicked is wrath.

24 There is that scattereth, and yout increaseth; and there is that withholdeth more than is meet, but it tendeth to poverty.

25 The liberal soul shall be made fat: and he that watereth shall be watered also himself.

26 He that withholdeth corn, the people shall curse him: but blessing shall be upon the head of him that selleth it.

27 He that diligently seeketh good procureth favour: but he that seeketh mischief, it shall come unto him.

Day 11

28 He that trusteth in his riches shall fall; but the righteous shall flourish as a branch.

29 He that troubleth his own house shall inherit the wind: and the fool shall be servant to the wise of heart.

30 The fruit of the righteous is a tree of life; and he that winneth souls is wise.

31 Behold, the righteous shall be recompensed in the earth: much more the wicked and the sinner.

Day 11

Day 12

"The best students of life are not determined by how they ask questions but in how they respond to the answers." ~ Dr Will

Psalms 56

Be merciful unto me, O GOD: for man would swallow me up; he fighting daily oppresseth me.

2 Mine enemies would daily swallow me up: for they be many that fight against me, O thou most High.

3 What time I am afraid, I will trust in thee.

4 In GOD I will praise his word, in GOD I have put my trust; I will not fear what flesh can do unto me.

5 Every day they wrest my words: all their thoughts are against me for evil.

6 They gather themselves together, they hide themselves, they mark
my steps, when they wait for my soul.

7 Shall they escape by iniquity? in thine anger cast down the people, O GOD.

Day 12

8 Thou tellest my wanderings: put thou my tears into thy bottle: are they not in thy book?

9 When I cry unto thee, then shall mine enemies turn back: this I know; for GOD is for me.

10 In GOD will I praise his word: in the Lord will I praise his word.

11 In GOD have I put my trust: I will not be afraid what man can do unto me.

12 Thy vows are upon me, O GOD: I will render praises unto thee.

13 For thou hast delivered my soul from death: wilt not thou deliver my feet from falling, that I may walk before GOD in the light of the living?

Psalms 57

Be merciful unto me, O GOD, be merciful unto me: for my soul trusteth in thee: yea, in the shadow of thy wings will I make my refuge, until these calamities be overpast.

2 I will cry unto GOD most high; unto GOD that performeth all things for me.

3 He shall send from heaven, and save me from the reproach of him that would swallow me up. Selah. GOD shall send forth his mercy and his truth.

4 My soul is among lions: and I lie even among them that are set on fire, even the sons of men, whose teeth are spears and arrows, and their tongue a sharp sword.

5 Be thou exalted, O GOD, above the heavens; let thy glory be above all the earth.

6 They have prepared a net for my steps; my soul is bowed down: they have digged a pit before me, into the midst whereof they are fallen themselves. Selah.

7 My heart is fixed, O GOD, my heart is fixed: I will sing and give praise.

8 Awake up, my glory; awake, psaltery and harp: I myself will awake early.

9 I will praise thee, O Lord, among the people: I will sing unto thee among the nations.

10 For thy mercy is great unto the heavens, and thy truth unto the clouds.

11 Be thou exalted, O GOD, above the heavens: let thy glory be above all the earth.

Psalms 58

Do ye indeed speak righteousness, O congregation? do ye judge uprightly, O ye sons of men?

Day 12

2 Yea, in heart ye work wickedness; ye weigh the violence of your hands in the earth.

3 The wicked are estranged from the womb: they go astray as soon as they be born, speaking lies.

4 Their poison is like the poison of a serpent: they are like the deaf adder that stoppeth her ear;

5 Which will not hearken to the voice of charmers, charming never so wisely.

6 Break their teeth, O GOD, in their mouth: break out the great teeth of the young lions, O Lord.

7 Let them melt away as waters which run continually: when he bendeth his bow to shoot his arrows, let them be as cut in pieces.

8 As a snail which melteth, let every one of them pass away: like the untimely birth of a woman, that they may not see the sun.

9 Before your pots can feel the thorns, he shall take them away as with a whirlwind, both living, and in his wrath.

10 The righteous shall rejoice when he seeth the vengeance: he shall wash his feet in the blood of the wicked.

11 So that a man shall say, Verily there is a reward for the righteous: verily he is a GOD that judgeth in the earth.

Day 12

Psalms 59

Deliver me from mine enemies, O my GOD: defend me from them that rise up against me.

2 Deliver me from the workers of iniquity, and save me from bloody men.

3 For, lo, they lie in wait for my soul: the mighty are gathered against
me; not for my transgression, nor for my sin, O Lord.

4 They run and prepare themselves without my fault: awake to help me, and behold.

5 Thou therefore, O Lord GOD of hosts, the GOD of Israel, awake to visit all the heathen: be not merciful to any wicked transgressors. Selah.

6 They return at evening: they make a noise like a dog, and go round about the city.

7 Behold, they belch out with their mouth: swords are in their lips: for who, say they, doth hear?

8 But thou, O Lord, shalt laugh at them; thou shalt have all the heathen in derision.

9 Because of his strength will I wait upon thee: for GOD is my defence.

Day 12

10 The GOD of my mercy shall prevent me: GOD shall let me see my desire upon mine enemies.

11 Slay them not, lest my people forget: scatter them by thy power; and bring them down, O Lord our shield.

12 For the sin of their mouth and the words of their lips let them even be taken in their pride: and for cursing and lying which they speak.

13 Consume them in wrath, consume them, that they may not be: and let them know that GOD ruleth in Jacob unto the ends of the earth. Selah.

14 And at evening let them return; and let them make a noise like a dog, and go round about the city.

15 Let them wander up and down for meat, and grudge if they be not satisfied.

16 But I will sing of thy power; yea, I will sing aloud of thy mercy in the morning: for thou hast been my defence and refuge in the day of my trouble.

17 Unto thee, O my strength, will I sing: for GOD is my defence, and the GOD of my mercy.

Psalms 60

O GOD, you have cast us off, you have scattered us, you have been displeased; O turn yourself to us again.

Day 12

2 You have made the earth to tremble; you have broken it: heal the breaches thereof; for it shakes.

3 You have showed your people hard things: you have made us to drink the wine of astonishment.

4 You have given a banner to them that fear you, that it may be displayed because of the truth. Selah.

5 That your beloved may be delivered; save with your right hand, and hear me.

6 GOD has spoken in his holiness; I will rejoice, I will divide Shechem, and mete out the valley of Succoth.

7 Gilead is my, and Manasseh is my; Ephraim also is the strength of my head; Judah is my lawgiver;

8 Moab is my washpot; over Edom will I cast out my shoe: Philistia, triumph you because of me.

9 Who will bring me into the strong city? who will lead me into Edom?

10 Will not you, O GOD, which had cast us off? and you, O GOD, which did not go out with our armies?

11 Give us help from trouble: for vain is the help of man.

12 Through GOD we shall do valiantly: for he it is that shall tread down our enemies.

Day 12

Proverbs 12

Whoso loveth instruction loveth knowledge: but he that hateth reproof is brutish.

2 A good man obtaineth favour of the Lord: but a man of wicked devices will he condemn.

3 A man shall not be established by wickedness: but the root of the righteous shall not be moved.

4 A virtuous woman is a crown to her husband: but she that maketh ashamed is as rottenness in his bones.

5 The thoughts of the righteous are right: but the counsels of the wicked are deceit.

6 The words of the wicked are to lie in wait for blood: but the mouth of the upright shall deliver them.

7 The wicked are overthrown, and are not: but the house of the righteous shall stand.

8 A man shall be commended according to his wisdom: but he that is of a perverse heart shall be despised.

9 He that is despised, and has a servant, is better than he that honoureth himself, and lacketh bread.

10 A righteous man regardeth the life of his beast: but the tender mercies of the wicked are cruel.

11 He that tilleth his land shall be satisfied with bread: but he that followeth vain persons is void of understanding.

12 The wicked desireth the net of evil men: but the root of the righteous yieldeth fruit.

13 The wicked is snared by the transgression of his lips: but the just shall come out of trouble.

14 A man shall be satisfied with good by the fruit of his mouth: and the recompence of a man's hands shall be rendered unto him.

15 The way of a fool is right in his own eyes: but he that hearkeneth unto counsel is wise.

16 A fool's wrath is presently known: but a prudent man covereth shame.

17 He that speaketh truth sheweth forth righteousness: but a false witness deceit.

18 There is that speaketh like the piercings of a sword: but the tongue of the wise is health.

19 The lip of truth shall be established for ever: but a lying tongue is but for a moment.

20 Deceit is in the heart of them that imagine evil: but to the counsellors of peace is joy.

21 There shall no evil happen to the just: but the wicked shall be filled with mischief.

22 Lying lips are abomination to the Lord: but they that deal truly are his delight.

23 A prudent man concealeth knowledge: but the heart of fools proclaimeth foolishness.

24 The hand of the diligent shall bear rule: but the slothful shall be under tribute.

25 Heaviness in the heart of man maketh it stoop: but a good word maketh it glad.

26 The righteous is more excellent than his neighbour: but the way of the wicked seduceth them.

27 The slothful man roasteth not that which he took in hunting: but the substance of a diligent man is precious.

28 In the way of righteousness is life: and in the pathway thereof there is no death.

Day 13

"Whether you come to the alter or altar the purpose is to cause something in your life to change." ~ Dr Will

Psalms 61

Hear my cry, O GOD; attend unto my prayer.

2 From the end of the earth will I cry unto you, when my heart is overwhelmed: lead me to the rock that is higher than I.

3 For you have been a shelter for me and a strong tower from the enemy.

4 I will abide in your tabernacle forever: I will trust in the covert of your wings. Selah.

5 For you, O GOD, have heard my vows: you have given me the heritage of those that fear your name.

6 Your will prolong the king's life: and his years as many generations.

7 He shall abide before GOD forever: O prepare mercy and truth, which may preserve him.

8 So will I sing praise unto your name forever, that I may daily perform my vows.

Psalms 62

Truly my soul waits upon GOD: from him cometh my salvation.

2 He only is my rock and my salvation; he is my defense; I shall not be greatly moved.

3 How long will you imagine mischief against a man? you shall be slain all of you: as a bowing wall shall you be, and as a tottering fence.

4 They only consult to cast him down from his excellency: they delight in lies: they bless with their mouth, but they curse inwardly. Selah.

5 My soul, wait you only upon GOD; for my expectation is from him.

6 He only is my rock and my salvation: he is my defense; I shall not be moved.

7 In GOD is my salvation and my glory: the rock of my strength, and my refuge, is in GOD.

8 Trust in him at all times; you people, pour out your heart before him: GOD is a refuge for us. Selah.

9 Surely men of low degree are vanity, and men of high degree are a lie: to be laid in the balance, they are altogether lighter than vanity.

10 Trust not in oppression, and become not vain in robbery: if riches increase, set not your heart upon them.

11 GOD has spoken once; twice have I heard this; that power belongs unto GOD.

12 Also unto you, O Lord, belongs mercy: for you render to every man according to his work.

Psalms 63

O GOD, you are my GOD; early will I seek you: my soul thirsts for you, my flesh longs for you in a dry and thirsty land, where no water is;

2 To see your power and your glory, so as I have seen you in the sanctuary.

3 Because your loving kindness is better than life, my lips shall praise you.

4 Thus will I bless you while I live: I will lift up my hands in your name.

5 My soul shall be satisfied as with marrow and fatness; and my mouth shall praise you with joyful lips:

Day 13

6 When I remember you upon my bed, and meditate on you in the night watches.

7 Because you have been my help, therefore in the shadow of your wings will I rejoice.

8 My soul follows hard after you: your right hand upholds me.

9 But those that seek my soul, to destroy it, shall go into the lower pares of the earth.

10 They shall fall by the sword: they shall be a portion for foxes.

11 But the king shall rejoice in GOD; every one that swears by him shall glory: but the mouth of them that speak lies shall be stopped.

Psalms 64

Hear my voice, O GOD, in my prayer: preserve my life from fear of the enemy.

2 Hide me from the secret counsel of the wicked; from the insurrection of the workers of iniquity:

3 Who whet their tongue like a sword, and bend their bows to shoot their arrows, even bitter words:

Day 13

4 That they may shoot in secret at the perfect: suddenly do they shoot at him, and fear not.

5 They encourage themselves in an evil matter: they commune of laying snares privily; they say, Who shall see them?

6 They search out iniquities; they accomplish a diligent search: both the inward thought of every one of them, and the heart, is deep.

7 But GOD shall shoot at them with an arrow; suddenly shall they be wounded.

8 So they shall make their own tongue to fall upon themselves: all that see them shall flee away.

9 And all men shall fear, and shall declare the work of GOD; for they shall wisely consider of his doing.

10 The righteous shall be glad in the LORD, and shall trust in him; and all the upright in heart shall glory.

Psalms 65

Praise waits for you, O GOD, in Sion: and unto you shall the vow be performed.

2 O you that hears prayer, unto you shall all flesh come.

Day 13

3 Iniquities prevail against me: as for our transgressions, you shall purge them away.

4 Blessed is the man whom you choose, and cause to approach unto you, that he may dwell in your courts: we shall be satisfied with the goodness of your house, even of your holy temple.

5 By terrible things in righteousness will you answer us, O GOD of our salvation; who are the confidence of all the ends of the earth, and of them that are afar off upon the sea:

6 Which by his strength set fast the mountains; being girded with power:

7 Which stills the noise of the seas, the noise of their waves, and the
tumult of the people.

8 They also that dwell in the uttermost pares are afraid at your tokens: you make the outgoings of the morning and evening to rejoice.

9 You visit the earth, and water it: you greatly enrich it with the river of GOD, which is full of water: you prepare them corn, when you have so provided for it.

10 You water the ridges thereof abundantly: you settle the furrows thereof: you make it soft with showers: you bless the springing thereof.

Day 13

11 You crown the year with your goodness; and your paths drop fatness.

12 They drop upon the pastures of the wilderness: and the little hills rejoice on every side.

13 The pastures are clothed with flocks; the valleys also are covered over with corn; they shout for joy, they also sing.

Proverbs 13

A wise son heareth his father's instruction: but a scorner heareth not rebuke.

2 A man shall eat good by the fruit of his mouth: but the soul of the transgressors shall eat violence.

3 He that keepeth his mouth keepeth his life: but he that openeth wide his lips shall have destruction.

4 The soul of the sluggard desireth, and has nothing: but the soul of the diligent shall be made fat.

5 A righteous man hateth lying: but a wicked man is loathsome, and cometh to shame.

6 Righteousness keepeth him that is upright in the way: but wickedness overthroweth the sinner.

Day 13

7 There is that maketh himself rich, yout has nothing: there is that maketh himself poor, yout has great riches.

8 The ransom of a man's life are his riches: but the poor heareth not rebuke.

9 The light of the righteous rejoiceth: but the lamp of the wicked shall be put out.

10 Only by pride cometh contention: but with the well advised is wisdom.

11 Wealth gotten by vanity shall be diminished: but he that gathereth by labour shall increase.

12 Hope deferred maketh the heart sick: but when the desire cometh, it is a tree of life.

13 Whoso despiseth the word shall be destroyed: but he that feareth the commandment shall be rewarded.

14 The law of the wise is a fountain of life, to depart from the snares of death.

15 Good understanding giveth favour: but the way of transgressors is hard.

16 Every prudent man dealeth with knowledge: but a fool layouth open his folly.

17 A wicked messenger falleth into mischief: but a faithful ambassador is health.

18 Poverty and shame shall be to him that refuseth instruction: but he that regardeth reproof shall be honoured.

19 The desire accomplished is sweet to the soul: but it is abomination to fools to depart from evil.

20 He that walketh with wise men shall be wise: but a companion of fools shall be destroyed.

21 Evil pursueth sinners: but to the righteous good shall be repayoud.

22 A good man leaveth an inheritance to his children's children: and the wealth of the sinner is laid up for the just.

23 Much food is in the tillage of the poor: but there is that is destroyed for want of judgment.

24 He that spareth his rod hateth his son: but he that loveth him chasteneth him betimes.

25 The righteous eateth to the satisfying of his soul: but the belly of the wicked shall want.

Day 13

Day 14

"EGO = Edging GOD Out." ~ Dr Will

Psalms 66

Make a joyful noise unto GOD, all you lands:

2 Sing forth the honor of his name: make his praise glorious.

3 Say unto GOD, How terrible are your in your works! through the greatness of your power shall your enemies submit themselves unto you.

4 All the earth shall worship you, and shall sing unto you; they shall sing to your name. Selah.

5 Come and see the works of GOD: he is terrible in his doing toward the children of men.

6 He turned the sea into dry land: they went through the flood on foot: there did we rejoice in him.

7 He rules by his power forever; his eyes behold the nations: let not the rebellious exalt themselves. Selah.

8 O bless our GOD, you people, and make the voice of his praise to be heard:

Day 14

9 Which holds our soul in life, and suffers not our feet to be moved.

10 For you, O GOD, hast proved us: you have tried us, as silver is tried.

11 You brought us into the net; your laid affliction upon our loins.

12 You have caused men to ride over our heads; we went through fire and through water: but you brought us out into a wealthy place.

13 I will go into your house with burnt offerings: I will pay you my vows,

14 Which my lips have uttered, and my mouth has spoken, when I was in trouble.

15 I will offer unto you burnt sacrifices of fatlings, with the incense of rams; I will offer bullocks with goats. Selah.

16 Come and hear, all you that fear GOD, and I will declare what he has done for my soul.

17 I cried unto him with my mouth, and he was extolled with my tongue.

18 If I regard iniquity in my heart, the Lord will not hear me:

Day 14

19 But verily GOD has heard me; he has attended to the voice of my prayer.

20 Blessed be GOD, which has not turned away my prayer, nor his mercy from me.

Psalms 67

GOD be merciful unto us, and bless us; and cause his face to shine upon us; Selah.

2 That your way may be known upon earth, your saving health among all nations.

3 Let the people praise you, O GOD; let all the people praise you.

4 O let the nations be glad and sing for joy: for you shall judge the people righteously, and govern the nations upon earth. Selah.

5 Let the people praise you, O GOD; let all the people praise you.

6 Then shall the earth yield her increase; and GOD, even our own GOD, shall bless us.

7 GOD shall bless us; and all the ends of the earth shall fear him.

Day 14

Psalms 68

Let GOD arise, let his enemies be scattered: let them also that hate him flee before him.

2 As smoke is driven away, so drive them away: as wax melts before the fire, so let the wicked perish at the presence of GOD.

3 But let the righteous be glad; let them rejoice before GOD: yes, let them exceedingly rejoice.

4 Sing unto GOD, sing praises to his name: extol him that rides upon the heavens by his name JAH, and rejoice before him.

5 A father of the fatherless, and a judge of the widows, is GOD in his holy habitation.

6 GOD sets the solitary in families: he brings out those which are bound with chains: but the rebellious dwell in a dry land.

7 O GOD, when you went forth before your people, when you did march through the wilderness; Selah:

8 The earth shook, the heavens also dropped at the presence of GOD: even Sinai itself was moved at the presence of GOD, the GOD of Israel.

9 You, O GOD, did send a plentiful rain, whereby you did confirm your inheritance, when it was weary.

10 Your congregation has dwelt therein: you, O GOD, hast prepared of your goodness for the poor.

11 The Lord gave the word: great was the company of those that published it.

12 Kings of armies did flee apace: and she that tarried at home divided the spoil.

13 Though you have lien among the pots, yet shall you be as the wings of a dove covered with silver, and her feathers with yellow gold.

14 When the Almighty scattered kings in it, it was white as snow in
Salmon.

15 The hill of GOD is as the hill of Bashan; an high hill as the hill of Bashan.

16 Why leap you, you high hills? this is the hill which GOD desires to dwell in; yes, the LORD will dwell in it forever.

17 The chariots of GOD are twenty thousand, even thousands of angels: the Lord is among them, as in Sinai, in the holy place.

Day 14

18 You have ascended on high, you have led captivity captive: you have received gifts for men; yous, for the rebellious also, that the LORD GOD might dwell among them.

19 Blessed be the Lord, who daily loads us with benefits, even the GOD of our salvation. Selah.

20 He that is our GOD is the GOD of salvation; and unto GOD the Lord belong the issues from death.

21 But GOD shall wound the head of his enemies, and the hairy scalp of such an one as goes on still in his trespasses.

22 The Lord said, I will bring again from Bashan, I will bring my
people again from the depths of the sea:

23 That your foot may be dipped in the blood of your enemies, and the tongue of your dogs in the same.

24 They have seen your goings, O GOD; even the goings of my GOD, my King, in the sanctuary.

25 The singers went before, the players on instruments followed after; among them were the damsels playing with timbrels.

26 Bless you GOD in the congregations, even the Lord, from the fountain of Israel.

Day 14

27 There is little Benjamin with their ruler, the princes of Judah and their council, the princes of Zebulun, and the princes of Naphtali.

28 Your GOD has commanded your strength: strengthen, O GOD, that which you have wrought for us.

29 Because of your temple at Jerusalem shall kings bring presents unto you.

30 Rebuke the company of spearmen, the multitude of the bulls, with the calves of the people, till every one submit himself with pieces of silver: scatter you the people that delight in war.

31 Princes shall come out of Egypt; Ethiopia shall soon stretch out her hands unto GOD.

32 Sing unto GOD, you kingdoms of the earth; O sing praises unto the Lord; Selah:

33 To him that rides upon the heavens of heavens, which were of old; lo, he doth send out his voice, and that a mighty voice.

34 Ascribe you strength unto GOD: his excellency is over Israel, and his strength is in the clouds.

35 O GOD, you are terrible out of your holy places: the GOD of Israel is he that gives strength and power unto his people. Blessed be GOD.

Day 14

Psalms 69

Save me, O GOD; for the waters are come in unto my soul.

2 I sink in deep mire, where there is no standing: I am come into deep waters, where the floods overflow me.

3 I am weary of my crying: my throat is dried: my eyes fail while I wait for my GOD.

4 They that hate me without a cause are more than the hairs of my head: they that would destroy me, being my enemies wrongfully, are mighty: then I restored that which I took not away.

5 O GOD, you know my foolishness; and my sins are not hid from you.

6 Let not them that wait on you, O Lord GOD of hosts, be ashamed for my sake: let not those that seek you be confounded for my sake, O GOD of Israel.

7 Because for your sake I have borne reproach; shame has covered my face.

8 I am become a stranger unto my brethren, and an alien unto my mother's children.

9 For the zeal of your house has eaten me up; and the reproaches of them that reproached you are fallen upon me.

10 When I wept, and chastened my soul with fasting, that was to my reproach.

11 I made sackcloth also my garment; and I became a proverb to them.

12 They that sit in the gate speak against me; and I was the song of the drunkards.

13 But as for me, my prayer is unto you, O LORD, in an acceptable time: O GOD, in the multitude of your mercy hear me, in the truth of your salvation.

14 Deliver me out of the mire, and let me not sink: let me be delivered from them that hate me, and out of the deep waters.

15 Let not the water flood overflow me, neither let the deep swallow me up, and let not the pit shut her mouth upon me.

16 Hear me, O LORD; for your loving kindness is good: turn unto me according to the multitude of your tender mercies.

17 And hide not your face from your servant; for I am in trouble: hear me speedily.

18 Draw nigh unto my soul, and redeem it: deliver me because of my enemies.

Day 14

19 You have known my reproach, and my shame, and my dishonor: my adversaries are all before you.

20 Reproach has broken my heart; and I am full of heaviness: and I looked for some to take pity, but there was none; and for comforters, but I found none.

21 They gave me also gall for my meat; and in my thirst they gave me vinegar to drink.

22 Let their table become a snare before them: and that which should have been for their welfare, let it become a trap.

23 Let their eyes be darkened, that they see not; and make their loins
continually to shake.

24 Pour out your indignation upon them, and let your wrathful anger take hold of them.

25 Let their habitation be desolate; and let none dwell in their tents.

26 For they persecute him whom you have smitten; and they talk to the grief of those whom you have wounded.

27 Add iniquity unto their iniquity: and let them not come into your righteousness.

Day 14

28 Let them be blotted out of the book of the living, and not be written with the righteous.

29 But I am poor and sorrowful: let your salvation, O GOD, set me up on high.

30 I will praise the name of GOD with a song, and will magnify him with thanksgiving.

31 This also shall please the LORD better than an ox or bullock that has horns and hoofs.

32 The humble shall see this, and be glad: and your heart shall live that seek GOD.

33 For the LORD hears the poor, and despises not his prisoners.

34 Let the heaven and earth praise him, the seas, and everything that movestherein.

35 For GOD will save Zion, and will build the cities of Judah: that they may dwell there, and have it in possession.

36 The seed also of his servants shall inherit it: and they that love his name shall dwell therein.

Psalms 70

Make haste, O GOD, to deliver me; make haste to help me, O LORD.

Day 14

2 Let them be ashamed and confounded that seek after my soul: let them be turned backward, and put to confusion, that desire my hurt.

3 Let them be turned back for a reward of their shame that say, Aha, aha.

4 Let all those that seek you rejoice and be glad in you: and let such as love your salvation say continually, Let GOD be magnified.

5 But I am poor and needy: make haste unto me, O GOD: your are my help and my deliverer; O LORD, make no tarrying.

Proverbs 14

Every wise woman buildeth her house: but the foolish plucketh it down with her hands.

2 He that walketh in his uprightness feareth the Lord: but he that is perverse in his ways despiseth him.

3 In the mouth of the foolish is a rod of pride: but the lips of the wise shall preserve them.

4 Where no oxen are, the crib is clean: but much increase is by the strength of the ox.

5 A faithful witness will not lie: but a false witness will utter lies.

Day 14

6 A scorner seeketh wisdom, and findeth it not: but knowledge is easy unto him that understandeth.

7 Go from the presence of a foolish man, when you perceivest not in him the lips of knowledge.

8 The wisdom of the prudent is to understand his way: but the folly of fools is deceit.

9 Fools make a mock at sin: but among the righteous there is favour.

10 The heart knoweth his own bitterness; and a stranger doth not intermeddle with his joy.

11 The house of the wicked shall be overthrown: but the tabernacle of the upright shall flourish.

12 There is a way which seemeth right unto a man, but the end thereof are the ways of death.

13 Even in laughter the heart is sorrowful; and the end of that mirth is heaviness.

14 The backslider in heart shall be filled with his own ways: and a good man shall be satisfied from himself.

15 The simple believeth every word: but the prudent man looketh well to his going.

Day 14

16 A wise man feareth, and departeth from evil: but the fool rageth, and is confident.

17 He that is soon angry dealeth foolishly: and a man of wicked devices is hated.

18 The simple inherit folly: but the prudent are crowned with knowledge.

19 The evil bow before the good; and the wicked at the gates of the righteous.

20 The poor is hated even of his own neighbour: but the rich has many friends.

21 He that despiseth his neighbour sinneth: but he that has mercy on the poor, happy is he.

22 Do they not err that devise evil? but mercy and truth shall be to them that devise good.

23 In all labour there is profit: but the talk of the lips tendeth only to penury.

24 The crown of the wise is their riches: but the foolishness of fools is folly.

25 A true witness delivereth souls: but a deceitful witness speaketh lies.

26 In the fear of the Lord is strong confidence: and his children shall have a place of refuge.

27 The fear of the Lord is a fountain of life, to depart from the snares of death.

28 In the multitude of people is the king's honour: but in the want of people is the destruction of the prince.

29 He that is slow to wrath is of great understanding: but he that is hasty of spirit exalteth folly.

30 A sound heart is the life of the flesh: but envy the rottenness of the bones.

31 He that oppresseth the poor reproacheth his Maker: but he that honoureth him has mercy on the poor.

32 The wicked is driven away in his wickedness: but the righteous has hope in his death.

33 Wisdom resteth in the heart of him that has understanding: but that which is in the midst of fools is made known.

34 Righteousness exalteth a nation: but sin is a reproach to any people.

35 The king's favour is toward a wise servant: but his wrath is against him that causeth shame.

Day 14

Day 15

"Rashness is the parent of misfortune. I have never seen a man fall into misfortune that was not preceded by a hasty act." ~ Dr Will

Psalms 71

In you, O LORD, do I put my trust: let me never be put to confusion.

2 Deliver me in your righteousness, and cause me to escape: incline your ear unto me, and save me.

3 Be you my strong habitation, whereunto I may continually resort: you have given commandment to save me; for your are my rock and my fortress.

4 Deliver me, O my GOD, out of the hand of the wicked, out of the hand of the unrighteous and cruel man.

5 For you are my hope, O Lord GOD: you are my trust from my youth.

6 By you have I been held up from the womb: you are he that took me out of my mother's bowels: my praise shall be continually of you.

Day 15

7 I am as a wonder unto many; but you are my strong refuge.

8 Let my mouth be filled with your praise and with your honor all the day.

9 Cast me not off in the time of old age; forsake me not when my strength fails.

10 For my enemies speak against me; and they that lay wait for my soul take counsel together,

11 Saying, GOD has forsaken him: persecute and take him; for there is none to deliver him.

12 O GOD, be not far from me: O my GOD, make haste for my help.

13 Let them be confounded and consumed that are adversaries to my soul; let them be covered with reproach and dishonor that seek my hurt.

14 But I will hope continually, and will yet praise you more and more.

15 My mouth shall show forth your righteousness and your salvation all the day; for I know not the numbers thereof.

16 I will go in the strength of the Lord GOD: I will make mention of your righteousness, even of your only.

17 O GOD, you have taught me from my youth: and hitherto have I declared your wondrous works.

18 Now also when I am old and gray headed, O GOD, forsake me not; until I have showed your strength unto this generation, and your power to every one that is to come.

19 Your righteousness also, O GOD, is very high, who hast done great things: O GOD, who is like unto you!

20 Your, which hast showed me great and sore troubles, shall quicken me again, and shall bring me up again from the depths of the earth.

21 You shall increase my greatness, and comfort me on every side.

22 I will also praise you with the psaltery, even your truth, O my GOD: unto you will I sing with the harp, O your Holy One of Israel.

23 My lips shall greatly rejoice when I sing unto you; and my soul, which you have redeemed.

24 My tongue also shall talk of your righteousness all the day long: for they are confounded, for they are brought unto shame, that seek my hurt.

Day 15

Psalms 72

Give the king your judgments, O GOD, and your righteousness unto the king's son.

2 He shall judge your people with righteousness, and your poor with judgment.

3 The mountains shall bring peace to the people, and the little hills, by righteousness.

4 He shall judge the poor of the people, he shall save the children of the needy, and shall break in pieces the oppressor.

5 They shall fear you as long as the sun and moon endure, throughout all generations.

6 He shall come down like rain upon the mown grass: as showers that water the earth.

7 In his days shall the righteous flourish; and abundance of peace so long as the moon endures.

8 He shall have dominion also from sea to sea, and from the river unto the ends of the earth.

9 They that dwell in the wilderness shall bow before him; and his enemies shall lick the dust.

10 The kings of Tarshish and of the isles shall bring presents: the kings of Sheba and Seba shall offer gifts.

Day 15

11 Yes, all kings shall fall down before him: all nations shall serve him.

12 For he shall deliver the needy when he cries; the poor also, and him that has no helper.

13 He shall spare the poor and needy, and shall save the souls of the needy.

14 He shall redeem their soul from deceit and violence: and precious shall their blood be in his sight.

15 And he shall live, and to him shall be given of the gold of Sheba: prayer also shall be made for him continually; and daily shall he be praised.

16 There shall be a handful of corn in the earth upon the top of the mountains; the fruit thereof shall shake like Lebanon: and they of the city shall flourish like grass of the earth.

17 His name shall endure forever: his name shall be continued as long as the sun: and men shall be blessed in him: all nations shall call him blessed.

18 Blessed be the LORD GOD, the GOD of Israel, who only doeth wondrous things.

19 And blessed be his glorious name forever: and let the whole earth be filled with his glory; Amen, and Amen.

Day 15

20 The prayers of David the son of Jesse are ended.

Psalms 73

Truly GOD is good to Israel, even to such as are of a clean heart.

2 But as for me, my feet were almost gone; my steps had well nigh slipped.

3 For I was envious at the foolish, when I saw the prosperity of the wicked.

4 For there are no bands in their death: but their strength is firm.

5 They are not in trouble as other men; neither are they plagued like other men.

6 Therefore pride compasses them about as a chain; violence covers them as a garment.

7 Their eyes stand out with fatness: they have more than heart could wish.

8 They are corrupt, and speak wickedly concerning oppression: they speak loftily.

9 They set their mouth against the heavens, and their tongue walks through the earth.

10 Therefore his people return hither: and waters of a full cup are wrung out to them.

11 And they say, How doth GOD know? and is there knowledge in the most High?

12 Behold, these are the ungodly, who prosper in the world; they increase in riches.

13 Verily I have cleansed my heart in vain, and washed my hands in innocency.

14 For all the day long have I been plagued, and chastened every morning.

15 If I say, I will speak thus; behold, I should offend against the generation of your children.

16 When I thought to know this, it was too painful for me;

17 Until I went into the sanctuary of GOD; then understood I their end.

18 Surely you did set them in slippery places: you cast them down into destruction.

19 How are they brought into desolation, as in a moment! they are utterly consumed with terrors.

20 As a dream when one awake; so, O Lord, when you awake, you shall despise their image.

Day 15

21 Thus my heart was grieved, and I was pricked in my reins.

22 So foolish was I, and ignorant: I was as a beast before you.

23 Nevertheless I am continually with you: you have held me by my right hand.

24 You shall guide me with your counsel, and afterward receive me to glory.

25 Whom have I in heaven but you? and there is none upon earth that I desire beside you.

26 My flesh and my heart fails: but GOD is the strength of my heart, and my portion forever.

27 For, lo, they that are far from you shall perish: you have destroyed all them that go a whoring from you.

28 But it is good for me to draw near to GOD: I have put my trust in the Lord GOD, that I may declare all your works.

Psalms 74

O GOD, why hast you cast us off forever? why doth your anger smoke against the sheep of your pasture?

2 Remember your congregation, which you have purchased of old; the rod of your inheritance, which you have redeemed; this mount Zion, wherein you have dwelt.

3 Lift up your feet unto the perpetual desolations; even all that the enemy has done wickedly in the sanctuary.

4 Your enemies roar in the midst of your congregations; they set up their ensigns for signs.

5 A man was famous according as he had lifted up axes upon the thick trees.

6 But now they break down the carved work thereof at once with axes and hammers.

7 They have cast fire into your sanctuary, they have defiled by casting down the dwelling place of your name to the ground.

8 They said in their hearts, Let us destroy them together: they have burned up all the synagogues of GOD in the land.

9 We see not our signs: there is no more any prophet: neither is there among us any that knows how long.

10 O GOD, how long shall the adversary reproach? shall the enemy blaspheme your name forever?

Day 15

11 Why withdraw you your hand, even your right hand? pluck it out of your bosom.

12 For GOD is my King of old, working salvation in the midst of the earth.

13 You did divide the sea by your strength: your broke the heads of the dragons in the waters.

14 You broke the heads of leviathan in pieces, and gave him to be meat to the people inhabiting the wilderness.

15 You did cleave the fountain and the flood: your dried up mighty rivers.

16 The day is yours, the night also is yours: you have prepared the light and the sun.

17 You have set all the borders of the earth: you have made summer and winter.

18 Remember this, that the enemy has reproached, O LORD, and that the foolish people have blasphemed your name.

19 O deliver not the soul of your turtledove unto the multitude of the wicked: forget not the congregation of your poor forever.

20 Have respect unto the covenant: for the dark places of the earth are full of the habitations of cruelty.

Day 15

21 O let not the oppressed return ashamed: let the poor and needy praise your name.

22 Arise, O GOD, plead your own cause: remember how the foolish man reproached you daily.

23 Forget not the voice of your enemies: the tumult of those that rise up against you increase continually.

Psalms 75

Unto you, O GOD, do we give thanks, unto you do we give thanks: for that your name is near your wondrous works declare.

2 When I shall receive the congregation I will judge uprightly.

3 The earth and all the inhabitants thereof are dissolved: I bear up the pillars of it. Selah.

4 I said unto the fools, Deal not foolishly: and to the wicked, Lift not up the horn:

5 Lift not up your horn on high: speak not with a stiff neck.

6 For promotion cometh neither from the east, nor from the west, nor from the south.

7 But GOD is the judge: he puts down one, and sets up another.

Day 15

8 For in the hand of the LORD there is a cup, and the wine is red; it is full of mixture; and he pours out of the same: but the dregs thereof, all the wicked of the earth shall wring them out, and drink them.

9 But I will declare forever; I will sing praises to the GOD of Jacob.

10 All the horns of the wicked also will I cut off; but the horns of the righteous shall be exalted.

Proverbs 15

15 A soft answer turneth away wrath: but grievous words stir up anger.

2 The tongue of the wise useth knowledge aright: but the mouth of fools poureth out foolishness.

3 The eyes of the Lord are in every place, beholding the evil and the good.

4 A wholesome tongue is a tree of life: but perverseness therein is a
breach in the spirit.

5 A fool despiseth his father's instruction: but he that regardeth reproof is prudent.

6 In the house of the righteous is much treasure: but in the revenues of the wicked is trouble.

7 The lips of the wise disperse knowledge: but the heart of the foolish doeth not so.

8 The sacrifice of the wicked is an abomination to the Lord: but the prayour of the upright is his delight.

9 The way of the wicked is an abomination unto the Lord: but he loveth him that followeth after righteousness.

10 Correction is grievous unto him that forsaketh the way: and he that hateth reproof shall die.

11 Hell and destruction are before the Lord: how much more then the hearts of the children of men?

12 A scorner loveth not one that reproveth him: neither will he go unto the wise.

13 A merry heart maketh a cheerful countenance: but by sorrow of the heart the spirit is broken.

14 The heart of him that has understanding seeketh knowledge: but the mouth of fools feedeth on foolishness.

15 All the days of the afflicted are evil: but he that is of a merry heart has a continual feast.

16 Better is little with the fear of the Lord than great treasure and trouble therewith.

Day 15

17 Better is a dinner of herbs where love is, than a stalled ox and hatred therewith.

18 A wrathful man stirreth up strife: but he that is slow to anger appeaseth strife.

19 The way of the slothful man is as an hedge of thorns: but the way of the righteous is made plain.

20 A wise son maketh a glad father: but a foolish man despiseth his mother.

21 Folly is joy to him that is destitute of wisdom: but a man of understanding walketh uprightly.

22 Without counsel purposes are disappointed: but in the multitude of counsellors they are established.

23 A man has joy by the answer of his mouth: and a word spoken in due season, how good is it!

24 The way of life is above to the wise, that he may depart from hell beneath.

25 The Lord will destroy the house of the proud: but he will establish the border of the widow.

26 The thoughts of the wicked are an abomination to the Lord: but the words of the pure are pleasant words.

27 He that is greedy of gain troubleth his own house; but he that hateth gifts shall live.

28 The heart of the righteous studieth to answer: but the mouth of the wicked poureth out evil things.

29 The Lord is far from the wicked: but he heareth the prayour of the righteous.

30 The light of the eyes rejoiceth the heart: and a good report maketh the bones fat.

31 The ear that heareth the reproof of life abideth among the wise.

32 He that refuseth instruction despiseth his own soul: but he that heareth reproof getteth understanding.

33 The fear of the Lord is the instruction of wisdom; and before honour is humility.

Day 15

Day 16

"Integrity is the ability to remain one with GOD even when you are under intense temptation and pressure. Integrity is the essence of excellence." ~ Dr Will

Psalms 76

In Judah is GOD known: his name is great in Israel.

2 In Salem also is his tabernacle, and his dwelling place in Zion.

3 There brake he the arrows of the bow, the shield, and the sword, and the battle. Selah

4 You are more glorious and excellent than the mountains of prey.

5 The stouthearted are spoiled, they have slept their sleep: and none of the men of might have found their hands.

6 At your rebuke, O GOD of Jacob, both the chariot and horse are cast into a dead sleep.

7 You, even your, are to be feared: and who may stand in your sight when once you are angry?

8 Your did cause judgment to be heard from heaven; the earth feared, and was still,

9 When GOD arose to judgment, to save all the meek of the earth. Selah.

10 Surely the wrath of man shall praise you: the remainder of wrath shall your restrain.

11 Vow, and pay unto the LORD your GOD: let all that be round about him bring presents unto him that ought to be feared.

12 He shall cut off the spirit of princes: he is terrible to the kings of the earth.

Psalms 77

I cried unto GOD with my voice, even unto GOD with my voice; and he gave ear unto me.

2 In the day of my trouble I sought the Lord: my sore ran in the night, and ceased not: my soul refused to be comforted.

3 I remembered GOD, and was troubled: I complained, and my spirit was overwhelmed. Selah.

4 You hold my eyes waking: I am so troubled that I cannot speak.

Day 16

5 I have considered the days of old, the years of ancient times.

6 I call to remembrance my song in the night: I commune with my own heart: and my spirit made diligent search.

7 Will the Lord cast off forever? and will he be favorable no more?

8 Is his mercy clean gone forever? doth his promise fail forevermore?

9 Has GOD forgotten to be gracious? has he in anger shut up his tender mercies? Selah.

10 And I said, This is my infirmity: but I will remember the years of the right hand of the most High.

11 I will remember the works of the LORD: surely I will remember your wonders of old.

12 I will meditate also of all your work, and talk of your doings.

13 Your way, O GOD, is in the sanctuary: who is so great a GOD as our GOD?

14 Your are the GOD that doest wonders: you have declared your strength among the people.

Day 16

15 You have with your arm redeemed your people, the sons of Jacob and Joseph. Selah.

16 The waters saw you, O GOD, the waters saw you; they were afraid: the depths also were troubled.

17 The clouds poured out water: the skies sent out a sound: your arrows also went abroad.

18 The voice of your thunder was in the heaven: the lightning lightened the world: the earth trembled and shook.

19 Your way is in the sea, and your path in the great waters, and your footsteps are not known.

20 Your led your people like a flock by the hand of Moses and Aaron.

Psalms 78

Give ear, O my people, to my law: incline your ears to the words of my mouth.

2 I will open my mouth in a parable: I will utter dark sayings of old:

3 Which we have heard and known, and our fathers have told us.

4 We will not hide them from their children, showing to the generation to come the praises of the LORD, and his strength, and his wonderful works that he has done.

5 For he established a testimony in Jacob, and appointed a law in Israel, which he commanded our fathers, that they should make them known to their children:

6 That the generation to come might know them, even the children which should be born; who should arise and declare them to their children:

7 That they might set their hope in GOD, and not forget the works of GOD, but keep his commandments:

8 And might not be as their fathers, a stubborn and rebellious generation; a generation that set not their heart aright, and whose spirit was not steadfast with GOD.

9 The children of Ephraim, being armed, and carrying bows, turned back in the day of battle.

10 They kept not the covenant of GOD, and refused to walk in his law;

11 And forgot his works, and his wonders that he had showed them.

12 Marvelous things did he in the sight of their fathers, in the land of Egypt, in the field of Zoan.

Day 16

13 He divided the sea, and caused them to pass through; and he made the waters to stand as an heap.

14 In the daytime also he led them with a cloud, and all the night with a light of fire.

15 He clave the rocks in the wilderness, and gave them drink as out of the great depths.

16 He brought streams also out of the rock, and caused waters to run down like rivers.

17 And they sinned yet more against him by provoking the most High in the wilderness.

18 And they tempted GOD in their heart by asking meat for their lust.

19 Yes, they spoke against GOD; they said, Can GOD furnish a table in the wilderness?

20 Behold, he smote the rock, that the waters gushed out, and the streams overflowed; can he give bread also? can he provide flesh for his people?

21 Therefore the LORD heard this, and was wroth: so a fire was kindled against Jacob, and anger also came up against Israel;

22 Because they believed not in GOD, and trusted not in his salvation:

Day 16

23 Though he had commanded the clouds from above, and opened the doors of heaven,

24 And had rained down manna upon them to eat, and had given them of the corn of heaven.

25 Man did eat angels' food: he sent them meat to the full.

26 He caused an east wind to blow in the heaven: and by his power he brought in the south wind.

27 He rained flesh also upon them as dust, and feathered fowls like
as the sand of the sea:

28 And he let it fall in the midst of their camp, round about their habitations.

29 So they did eat, and were well filled: for he gave them their own desire;

30 They were not estranged from their lust. But while their meat was yout in their mouths,

31 The wrath of GOD came upon them, and slew the fattest of them,
and smote down the chosen men of Israel.

32 For all this they sinned still, and believed not for his wondrous works.

Day 16

33 Therefore their days did he consume in vanity, and their years in trouble.

34 When he slew them, then they sought him: and they returned and inquired early after GOD.

35 And they remembered that GOD was their rock, and the high GOD their redeemer.

36 Nevertheless they did flatter him with their mouth, and they lied unto him with their tongues.

37 For their heart was not right with him, neither were they steadfast in his covenant.

38 But he, being full of compassion, forgave their iniquity, and destroyed them not: yes, many a time turned he his anger away, and did not stir up all his wrath.

39 For he remembered that they were but flesh; a wind that passes away, and cometh not again.

40 How oft did they provoke him in the wilderness, and grieve him in the desert!

41 Yes, they turned back and tempted GOD, and limited the Holy One of Israel.

42 They remembered not his hand, nor the day when he delivered them from the enemy.

43 How he had wrought his signs in Egypt, and his wonders in the field of Zoan:

44 And had turned their rivers into blood; and their floods, that they could not drink.

45 He sent divers sorts of flies among them, which devoured them; and frogs, which destroyed them.

46 He gave also their increase unto the caterpillar, and their labor unto the locust.

47 He destroyed their vines with hail, and their sycamore trees with frost.

48 He gave up their cattle also to the hail, and their flocks to hot thunderbolts.

49 He cast upon them the fierceness of his anger, wrath, and indignation, and trouble, by sending evil angels among them.

50 He made a way to his anger; he spared not their soul from death, but gave their life over to the pestilence;

51 And smote all the firstborn in Egypt; the chief of their strength in the tabernacles of Ham:

52 But made his own people to go forth like sheep, and guided them in the wilderness like a flock.

Day 16

53 And he led them on safely, so that they feared not: but the sea overwhelmed their enemies.

54 And he brought them to the border of his sanctuary, even to this mountain, which his right hand had purchased.

55 He cast out the heathen also before them, and divided them an inheritance by line, and made the tribes of Israel to dwell in their tents.

56 Yet they tempted and provoked the Most High GOD, and kept not his testimonies:

57 But turned back, and dealt unfaithfully like their fathers: they were turned aside like a deceitful bow.

58 For they provoked him to anger with their high places, and moved him to jealousy with their graven images.

59 When GOD heard this, he was wroth, and greatly abhorred Israel:

60 So that he forsook the tabernacle of Shiloh, the tent which he placed among men;

61 And delivered his strength into captivity, and his glory into the enemy's hand.

62 He gave his people over also unto the sword; and was wroth with his inheritance.

63 The fire consumed their young men; and their maidens were not given to marriage.

64 Their priests fell by the sword; and their widows made no lamentation.

65 Then the Lord awaked as one out of sleep, and like a mighty man that shouted by reason of wine.

66 And he smote his enemies in the hinder pares: he put them to a perpetual reproach.

67 Moreover he refused the tabernacle of Joseph, and chose not the tribe of Ephraim:

68 But chose the tribe of Judah, the mount Zion which he loved.

69 And he built his sanctuary like high palaces, like the earth which he has established forever.

70 He chose David also his servant, and took him from the sheepfolds:

71 From following the ewes great with young he brought him to feed Jacob his people, and Israel his inheritance.

72 So he fed them according to the integrity of his heart; and guided them by the skillfulness of his hands.

Day 16

Psalms 79

O GOD, the heathen are come into your inheritance; your holy temple have they defiled; they have laid Jerusalem on heaps.

2 The dead bodies of your servants have they given to be meat unto the fowls of the heaven, the flesh of your saints unto the beasts of the earth.

3 Their blood have they shed like water round about Jerusalem; and there was none to bury them.

4 We are become a reproach to our neighbors, a scorn and derision to them that are round about us.

5 How long, LORD? will you be angry forever? shall your jealousy burn like fire?

6 Pour out your wrath upon the heathen that have not known you, and upon the kingdoms that have not called upon your name.

7 For they have devoured Jacob, and laid waste his dwelling place.

8 O remember not against us former iniquities: let your tender mercies speedily prevent us: for we are brought very low.

Day 16

9 Help us, O GOD of our salvation, for the glory of your name: and deliver us, and purge away our sins, for your name's sake.

10 Wherefore should the heathen say, Where is their GOD? let him be known among the heathen in our sight by the revenging of the blood of your servants which is shed.

11 Let the sighing of the prisoner come before you; according to the greatness of your power preserve you those that are appointed to die;

12 And render unto our neighbors sevenfold into their bosom their reproach, wherewith they have reproached you, O Lord.

13 So we your people and sheep of your pasture will give you thanks forever: we will show forth your praise to all generations.

Psalms 80

Give ear, O Shepherd of Israel, you that lead Joseph like a flock; your that dwells between the cherubims, shine forth.

2 Before Ephraim and Benjamin and Manasseh stir up your strength, and come and save us.

3 Turn us again, O GOD, and cause your face to shine; and we shall be saved.

Day 16

4 O LORD GOD of hosts, how long will you be angry against the prayer of your people?

5 You feed them with the bread of tears; and give them tears to drink in great measure.

6 You make us a strife unto our neighbors: and our enemies laugh among themselves.

7 Turn us again, O GOD of hosts, and cause your face to shine; and we shall be saved.

8 You have brought a vine out of Egypt: you have cast out the heathen, and planted it.

9 You prepared room before it, and did cause it to take deep root, and it filled the land.

10 The hills were covered with the shadow of it, and the boughs thereof were like the goodly cedars.

11 She sent out her boughs unto the sea, and her branches unto the river.

12 Why hast you then broken down her hedges, so that all they which pass by the way do pluck her?

13 The boar out of the wood doth waste it, and the wild beast of the field doth devour it.

14 Return, we beseech you, O GOD of hosts: look down from heaven, and behold, and visit this vine;

15 And the vineyard which your right hand has planted, and the branch that you made strong for yourself.

16 It is burned with fire, it is cut down: they perish at the rebuke of your countenance.

17 Let your hand be upon the man of your right hand, upon the son of man whom you made strong for yourself.

18 So will not we go back from you: quicken us, and we will call upon your name.

19 Turn us again, O LORD GOD of hosts, cause your face to shine; and we shall be saved.

Proverbs 16

16 The preparations of the heart in man, and the answer of the tongue, is from the Lord.

2 All the ways of a man are clean in his own eyes; but the Lord weigheth the spirits.

3 Commit your works unto the Lord, and your thoughts shall be established.

4 The Lord has made all things for himself: yea, even the wicked for the day of evil.

Day 16

5 Every one that is proud in heart is an abomination to the Lord: yough hand join in hand, he shall not be unpunished.

6 By mercy and truth iniquity is purged: and by the fear of the Lord men depart from evil.

7 When a man's ways please the Lord, he maketh even his enemies to be at peace with him.

8 Better is a little with righteousness than great revenues without right.

9 A man's heart deviseth his way: but the Lord directeth his steps.

10 A divine sentence is in the lips of the king: his mouth transgresseth not in judgment.

11 A just weight and balance are the Lord's: all the weights of the bag are his work.

12 It is an abomination to kings to commit wickedness: for the throne is established by righteousness.

13 Righteous lips are the delight of kings; and they love him that speaketh right.

14 The wrath of a king is as messengers of death: but a wise man will pacify it.

15 In the light of the king's countenance is life; and his favour is as a cloud of the latter rain.

16 How much better is it to get wisdom than gold! and to get understanding rather to be chosen than silver!

17 The highway of the upright is to depart from evil: he that keepeth his way preserveth his soul.

18 Pride goeth before destruction, and an haughty spirit before a fall.

19 Better it is to be of an humble spirit with the lowly, than to divide the spoil with the proud.

20 He that handleth a matter wisely shall find good: and whoso trusteth in the Lord, happy is he.

21 The wise in heart shall be called prudent: and the sweetness of the lips increaseth learning.

22 Understanding is a wellspring of life unto him that has it: but the instruction of fools is folly.

23 The heart of the wise teacheth his mouth, and addeth learning to his lips.

24 Pleasant words are as an honeycomb, sweet to the soul, and health to the bones.

Day 16

25 There is a way that seemeth right unto a man, but the end thereof are the ways of death.

26 He that laboureth laboureth for himself; for his mouth craveth it of him.

27 An ungodly man diggeth up evil: and in his lips there is as a burning fire.

28 A froward man soweth strife: and a whisperer separateth chief friends.

29 A violent man enticeth his neighbour, and leadeth him into the way that is not good.

30 He shutteth his eyes to devise froward things: moving his lips he bringeth evil to pass.

31 The hoary head is a crown of glory, if it be found in the way of righteousness.

32 He that is slow to anger is better than the mighty; and he that ruleth his spirit than he that taketh a city.

33 The lot is cast into the lap; but the whole disposing thereof is of the Lord.

Day 17

"Going to church doesn't make you a Christian any more than going to a garage makes you an automobile."
~ Billy Sunday

Psalms 81

Sing aloud unto GOD our strength: make a joyful noise unto the GOD of Jacob.

2 Take a psalm, and bring hither the timbrel, the pleasant harp with the psaltery.

3 Blow up the trumpet in the new moon, in the time appointed, on our solemn feast day.

4 For this was a statute for Israel, and a law of the GOD of Jacob.

5 This he ordained in Joseph for a testimony, when he went out through the land of Egypt: where I heard a language that I understood not.

6 I removed his shoulder from the burden: his hands were delivered from the pots.

Day 17

7 You called in trouble, and I delivered you; I answered you in the secret place of thunder: I proved you at the waters of Meribah. Selah.

8 Hear, O my people, and I will testify unto you: O Israel, if your will hearken unto me;

9 There shall no strange GOD be in you; neither shall your worship any strange GOD.

10 I am the LORD your GOD, which brought you out of the land of Egypt: open your mouth wide, and I will fill it.

11 But my people would not hearken to my voice; and Israel would
none of me.

12 So I gave them up unto their own hearts' lust: and they walked in their own counsels.

13 Oh that my people had hearkened unto me, and Israel had walked in my ways!

14 I should soon have subdued their enemies, and turned my hand against their adversaries.

15 The haters of the LORD should have submitted themselves unto him: but their time should have endured forever.

16 He should have fed them also with the finest of the wheat: and with honey out of the rock should I have satisfied you.

Psalms 82

GOD stands in the congregation of the mighty; he judges among the GODs.

2 How long will you judge unjustly, and accept the persons of the wicked? Selah.

3 Defend the poor and fatherless: do justice to the afflicted and needy.

4 Deliver the poor and needy: rid them out of the hand of the wicked.

5 They know not, neither will they understand; they walk on in darkness: all the foundations of the earth are out of course.

6 I have said, You are GODs; and all of you are children of the most High.

7 But you shall die like men, and fall like one of the princes.

8 Arise, O GOD, judge the earth: for you shall inherit all nations.

Day 17

Psalms 83

Keep not your silence, O GOD: hold not your peace, and be not still, O GOD.

2 For, lo, your enemies make a tumult: and they that hate you have lifted up the head.

3 They have taken crafty counsel against your people, and consulted
against your hidden ones.

4 They have said, Come, and let us cut them off from being a nation; that the name of Israel may be no more in remembrance.

5 For they have consulted together with one consent: they are confederate against you:

6 The tabernacles of Edom, and the Ishmaelites; of Moab, and the Hagarenes;

7 Gebal, and Ammon, and Amalek; the Philistines with the inhabitants of Tyre;

8 Assur also is joined with them: they have helped the children of Lot. Selah.

9 Do unto them as unto the Midianites; as to Sisera, as to Jabin, at the brook of Kison:

10 Which perished at Endor: they became as dung for the earth.

11 Make their nobles like Oreb, and like Zeeb: yous, all their princes as Zebah, and as Zalmunna:

12 Who said, Let us take to ourselves the houses of GOD in possession.

13 O my GOD, make them like a wheel; as the stubble before the wind.

14 As the fire burns a wood, and as the flame sets the mountains on fire;

15 So persecute them with your tempest, and make them afraid with your storm.

16 Fill their faces with shame; that they may seek your name, O LORD.

17 Let them be confounded and troubled forever; yes, let them be put to shame, and perish:

18 That men may know that you, whose name alone is JEHOVAH, are the most high over all the earth.

Psalms 84

How amiable are your tabernacles, O LORD of hosts!

Day 17

2 My soul longs, yes, even faints for the courts of the LORD: my heart and my flesh cries out for the living GOD.

3 Yes, the sparrow has found an house, and the swallow a nest for herself, where she may lay her young, even your altars, O LORD of hosts, my King, and my GOD.

4 Blessed are they that dwell in your house: they will be still praising you. Selah.

5 Blessed is the man whose strength is in you; in whose heart are the ways of them.

6 Who passing through the valley of Baca make it a well; the rain also filled the pools.

7 They go from strength to strength, every one of them in Zion appears before GOD.

8 O LORD GOD of hosts, hear my prayer: give ear, O GOD of Jacob. Selah.

9 Behold, O GOD our shield, and look upon the face of your anointed.

10 For a day in your courts is better than a thousand. I had rather be a doorkeeper in the house of my GOD, than to dwell in the tents of wickedness.

11 For the LORD GOD is a sun and shield: the LORD will give grace and glory: no good thing will he withhold from them that walk uprightly.

12 O LORD of hosts, blessed is the man that trusts in you.

Psalms 85

LORD, you have been favorable unto your land: you have brought back the captivity of Jacob.

2 You have forgiven the iniquity of your people, you have covered all their sin. Selah.

3 You have taken away all your wrath: you have turned yourself from the fierceness of your anger.

4 Turn us, O GOD of our salvation, and cause your anger toward us to cease.

5 Will you be angry with us forever? will you draw out your anger to all generations?

6 Will you not revive us again: that your people may rejoice in you?

7 Show us your mercy, O LORD, and grant us your salvation.

Day 17

8 I will hear what GOD the LORD will speak: for he will speak peace unto his people, and to his saints: but let them not turn again to folly.

9 Surely his salvation is nigh them that fear him; that glory may dwell in our land.

10 Mercy and truth are met together; righteousness and peace have kissed each other.

11 Truth shall spring out of the earth; and righteousness shall look down from heaven.

12 Yes, the LORD shall give that which is good; and our land shall yield her increase.

13 Righteousness shall go before him; and shall set us in the way of his steps.

Proverbs 17

Better is a dry morsel and quietness therewith than an house full of sacrifices with strife.

2 A wise servant shall have rule over a son that causeth shame, and shall have part of the inheritance among the brethren.

3 The fining pot is for silver, and the furnace for gold: but the Lord trieth the hearts.

Day 17

4 A wicked doer giveth heed to false lips; and a liar giveth ear to a naughty tongue.

5 Whoso mocketh the poor reproacheth his Maker: and he that is glad at calamities shall not be unpunished.

6 Children's children are the crown of old men; and the glory of children are their fathers.

7 Excellent speech becometh not a fool: much less do lying lips a prince.

8 A gift is as a precious stone in the eyes of him that has it: whithersoever it turneth, it prospereth.

9 He that covereth a transgression seeketh love; but he that repeateth a matter separateth very friends.

10 A reproof entereth more into a wise man than an hundred stripes into a fool.

11 An evil man seeketh only rebellion: therefore a cruel messenger shall be sent against him.

12 Let a bear robbed of her whelps meet a man, rather than a fool in his folly.

13 Whoso rewardeth evil for good, evil shall not depart from his house.

Day 17

14 The beginning of strife is as when one letteth out water: therefore leave off contention, before it be meddled with.

15 He that justifieth the wicked, and he that condemneth the just, even they both are abomination to the Lord.

16 Wherefore is there a price in the hand of a fool to get wisdom, seeing he has no heart to it?

17 A friend loveth at all times, and a brother is born for adversity.

18 A man void of understanding striketh hands, and becometh surety in the presence of his friend.

19 He loveth transgression that loveth strife: and he that exalteth his gate seeketh destruction.

20 He that has a froward heart findeth no good: and he that has a perverse tongue falleth into mischief.

21 He that begetteth a fool doeth it to his sorrow: and the father of a fool has no joy.

22 A merry heart doeth good like a medicine: but a broken spirit drieth the bones.

23 A wicked man taketh a gift out of the bosom to pervert the ways of judgment.

24 Wisdom is before him that has understanding; but the eyes of a fool are in the ends of the earth.

25 A foolish son is a grief to his father, and bitterness to her that bare him.

26 Also to punish the just is not good, nor to strike princes for equity.

27 He that has knowledge spareth his words: and a man of understanding is of an excellent spirit.

28 Even a fool, when he holdeth his peace, is counted wise: and he that shutteth his lips is esteemed a man of understanding.

Day 17

Day 18

"The primary cause of adult suffering is in not knowing who you are, why you are here, or what you were created to be." ~ Dr Will

Psalms 86

Bow down your ear, O LORD, hear me: for I am poor and needy.

2 Preserve my soul; for I am holy: O your my GOD, save your servant that trusts in you.

3 Be merciful unto me, O Lord: for I cry unto you daily.

4 Rejoice the soul of your servant: for unto you, O Lord, do I lift up my soul.

5 For you, Lord, are good, and ready to forgive; and plenteous in mercy unto all them that call upon you.

6 Give ear, O LORD, unto my prayer; and attend to the voice of my supplications.

7 In the day of my trouble I will call upon you: for your will answer me.

Day 18

8 Among the GODs there is none like unto you, O Lord; neither are there any works like unto your works.

9 All nations whom you have made shall come and worship before you, O Lord; and shall glorify your name.

10 For you are great, and doest wondrous things: your are GOD alone.

11 Teach me your way, O LORD; I will walk in your truth: unite my heart to fear your name.

12 I will praise you, O Lord my GOD, with all my heart: and I will glorify your name forevermore.

13 For great is your mercy toward me: and you have delivered my soul from the lowest hell.

14 O GOD, the proud are risen against me, and the assemblies of
violent men have sought after my soul; and have not set you before them.

15 But you, O Lord, are a GOD full of compassion, and gracious, longsuffering, and plenteous in mercy and truth.

16 O turn unto me, and have mercy upon me; give your strength unto your servant, and save the son of your handmaid.

17 Show me a token for good; that they which hate me may see it, and be ashamed: because you, LORD, have helped me, and comforted me.

Psalms 87

His foundation is in the holy mountains.

2 The LORD loves the gates of Zion more than all the dwellings of Jacob.

3 Glorious things are spoken of you, O city of GOD. Selah.

4 I will make mention of Rahab and Babylon to them that know me: behold Philistia, and Tyre, with Ethiopia; this man was born there.

5 And of Zion it shall be said, This and that man was born in her: and the highest himself shall establish her.

6 The LORD shall count, when he writes up the people, that this man was born there. Selah.

7 As well the singers as the players on instruments shall be there: all my springs are in you.

Psalms 88

O LORD GOD of my salvation, I have cried day and night before you:

Day 18

2 Let my prayer come before you: incline your ear unto my cry;

3 For my soul is full of troubles: and my life draws nigh unto the grave.

4 I am counted with them that go down into the pit: I am as a man that has no strength:

5 Free among the dead, like the slain that lie in the grave, whom you remember no more: and they are cut off from your hand.

6 You have laid me in the lowest pit, in darkness, in the deeps.

7 Your wrath lies hard upon me, and you have afflicted me with all your waves. Selah.

8 You have put away my acquaintance far from me; you have made me an abomination unto them: I am shut up, and I cannot come forth.

9 My eye mourns by reason of affliction: LORD, I have called daily upon you, I have stretched out my hands unto you.

10 Will you show wonders to the dead? shall the dead arise and praise you? Selah.

Day 18

11 Shall your loving kindness be declared in the grave? or your faithfulness in destruction?

12 Shall your wonders be known in the dark? and your righteousness in the land of forgetfulness?

13 But unto you have I cried, O LORD; and in the morning shall my prayer prevent you.

14 LORD, why cast you off my soul? why hide you your face from me?

15 I am afflicted and ready to die from my youth up: while I suffer your terrors I am distracted.

16 Your fierce wrath goes over me; your terrors have cut me off.

17 They came round about me daily like water; they compassed me about together.

18 Lover and friend hast you put far from me, and my acquaintance into darkness.

Psalms 89

I will sing of the mercies of the LORD forever: with my mouth will
I make known your faithfulness to all generations.

Day 18

2 For I have said, Mercy shall be built up forever: your faithfulness shall you establish in the very heavens.

3 I have made a covenant with my chosen, I have sworn unto David my servant,

4 Your seed will I establish forever, and build up your throne to all generations. Selah.

5 And the heavens shall praise your wonders, O LORD: your faithfulness also in the congregation of the saints.

6 For who in the heaven can be compared unto the LORD? who among the sons of the mighty can be likened unto the LORD?

7 GOD is greatly to be feared in the assembly of the saints, and to be had in reverence of all them that are about him.

8 O LORD GOD of hosts, who is a strong LORD like unto you? or to your faithfulness round about you?

9 You rule the raging of the sea: when the waves thereof arise, your stillest them.

10 You have broken Rahab in pieces, as one that is slain; you have scattered your enemies with your strong arm.

11 The heavens are yours, the earth also is yours: as for the world and the fullness thereof, you have founded them.

12 The north and the south you have created them: Tabor and Hermon shall rejoice in your name.

13 You have a mighty arm: strong is your hand, and high is your right hand.

14 Justice and judgment are the habitation of your throne: mercy and truth shall go before your face.

15 Blessed is the people that know the joyful sound: they shall walk, O LORD, in the light of your countenance.

16 In your name shall they rejoice all the day: and in your righteousness shall they be exalted.

17 For you are the glory of their strength: and in your favor our horn shall be exalted.

18 For the LORD is our defense; and the Holy One of Israel is our king.

19 Then you spoke in vision to your holy one, and said, I have laid help upon one that is mighty; I have exalted one chosen out of the people.

20 I have found David my servant; with my holy oil have I anointed him:

21 With whom my hand shall be established: my arm also shall strengthen him.

Day 18

22 The enemy shall not exact upon him; nor the son of wickedness afflict him.

23 And I will beat down his foes before his face, and plague them that hate him.

24 But my faithfulness and my mercy shall be with him: and in my name shall his horn be exalted.

25 I will set his hand also in the sea, and his right hand in the rivers.

26 He shall cry unto me, You are my father, my GOD, and the rock of my salvation.

27 Also I will make him my firstborn, higher than the kings of the earth.

28 My mercy will I keep for him forevermore, and my covenant shall stand fast with him.

29 His seed also will I make to endure forever, and his throne as the days of heaven.

30 If his children forsake my law, and walk not in my judgments;

31 If they break my statutes, and keep not my commandments;

Day 18

32 Then will I visit their transgression with the rod, and their iniquity with stripes.

33 Nevertheless my loving kindness will I not utterly take from him, nor suffer my faithfulness to fail.

34 My covenant will I not break, nor alter the thing that is gone out of my lips.

35 Once have I sworn by my holiness that I will not lie unto David.

36 His seed shall endure forever, and his throne as the sun before me.

37 It shall be established forever as the moon, and as a faithful witness in heaven. Selah.

38 But you have cast off and abhorred, you have been wroth with your anointed.

39 You have made void the covenant of your servant: you have profaned his crown by casting it to the ground.

40 You have broken down all his hedges; you have brought his strong holds to ruin.

41 All that pass by the way spoil him: he is a reproach to his neighbors.

Day 18

42 You have set up the right hand of his adversaries; you have made all his enemies to rejoice.

43 You have also turned the edge of his sword, and hast not made him to stand in the battle.

44 You have made his glory to cease, and cast his throne down to the ground.

45 The days of his youth hast your shortened: you have covered him with shame. Selah.

46 How long, LORD? will your hide yourself forever? shall your wrath burn like fire?

47 Remember how short my time is: wherefore hast your made all men in vain?

48 What man is he that liveth, and shall not see death? shall he deliver his soul from the hand of the grave? Selah.

49 Lord, where are your former loving kindnesses, which you swore
unto David in your truth?

50 Remember, Lord, the reproach of your servants; how I do bear in my bosom the reproach of all the mighty people;

51 Wherewith your enemies have reproached, O LORD; wherewith they have reproached the footsteps of your anointed.

52 Blessed be the LORD forevermore. Amen, and Amen.

Psalms 90

LORD, you have been our dwelling place in all generations.

2 Before the mountains were brought forth, or ever your had formed the earth and the world, even from everlasting to everlasting, your are GOD.

3 You turn man to destruction; and say, Return, you children of men.

4 For a thousand years in your sight are but as yesterday when it is past, and as a watch in the night.

5 You carry them away as with a flood; they are as a sleep: in the morning they are like grass which grows up.

6 In the morning it flourishes, and grows up; in the evening it is cut down, and withers.

7 For we are consumed by your anger, and by your wrath are we troubled.

8 You have set our iniquities before you, our secret sins in the light of your countenance.

9 For all our days are passed away in your wrath: we spend our years as a tale that is told.

Day 18

10 The days of our years are threescore years and ten; and if by reason of strength they be fourscore years, yet is their strength labor and sorrow; for it is soon cut off, and we fly away.

11 Who knows the power of your anger? even according to your fear, so is your wrath.

12 So teach us to number our days, that we may apply our hearts unto wisdom.

13 Return, O LORD, how long? and let it repent you concerning your servants.

14 O satisfy us early with your mercy; that we may rejoice and be glad all our days.

15 Make us glad according to the days wherein you have afflicted us, and the years wherein we have seen evil.

16 Let your work appear unto your servants, and your glory unto their children.

17 And let the beauty of the LORD our GOD be upon us: and establish you the work of our hands upon us; yes, the work of our hands establish you it.

Proverbs 18

Through desire a man, having separated himself, seeketh and intermeddleth with all wisdom.

Day 18

2 A fool has no delight in understanding, but that his heart may discover itself.

3 When the wicked cometh, then cometh also contempt, and with ignominy reproach.

4 The words of a man's mouth are as deep waters, and the wellspring of wisdom as a flowing brook.

5 It is not good to accept the person of the wicked, to overthrow the righteous in judgment.

6 A fool's lips enter into contention, and his mouth calleth for strokes.

7 A fool's mouth is his destruction, and his lips are the snare of his soul.

8 The words of a talebearer are as wounds, and they go down into the innermost parts of the belly.

9 He also that is slothful in his work is brother to him that is a great waster.

10 The name of the Lord is a strong tower: the righteous runneth into it, and is safe.

11 The rich man's wealth is his strong city, and as an high wall in his own conceit.

Day 18

12 Before destruction the heart of man is haughty, and before honour is humility.

13 He that answereth a matter before he heareth it, it is folly and shame unto him.

14 The spirit of a man will sustain his infirmity; but a wounded spirit who can bear?

15 The heart of the prudent getteth knowledge; and the ear of the wise seeketh knowledge.

16 A man's gift maketh room for him, and bringeth him before great men.

17 He that is first in his own cause seemeth just; but his neighbour cometh and searcheth him.

18 The lot causeth contentions to cease, and parteth between the mighty.

19 A brother offended is harder to be won than a strong city: and their contentions are like the bars of a castle.

20 A man's belly shall be satisfied with the fruit of his mouth; and with the increase of his lips shall he be filled.

21 Death and life are in the power of the tongue: and they that love it shall eat the fruit thereof.

22 Whoso findeth a wife findeth a good thing, and obtaineth favour of the Lord.

23 The poor useth intreaties; but the rich answereth roughly.

24 A man that has friends must shew himself friendly: and there is a friend that sticketh closer than a brother.

Day 18

Day 19

"For Christ is not entered into the holy places made with hands, which are the figures of the true… (Hebrews 9:24)."

Psalms 91

He that dwells in the secret place of the most High shall abide under the shadow of the Almighty.

2 I will say of the LORD, He is my refuge and my fortress: my GOD; in him will I trust.

3 Surely he shall deliver you from the snare of the fowler, and from the noisome pestilence.

4 He shall cover you with his feathers, and under his wings shall your trust: his truth shall be your shield and buckler.

5 You shall not be afraid for the terror by night; nor for the arrow that flies by day;

6 Nor for the pestilence that walk in darkness; nor for the destruction that waste at noonday.

7 A thousand shall fall at your side, and ten thousand at your right hand; but it shall not come nigh you.

Day 19

8 Only with your eyes shall you behold and see the reward of the wicked.

9 Because you have made the LORD, which is my refuge, even the most High, your habitation;

10 There shall no evil befall you, neither shall any plague come nigh your dwelling.

11 For he shall give his angels charge over you, to keep you in all your ways.

12 They shall bear you up in their hands, lest your dash your foot against a stone.

13 You shall tread upon the lion and adder: the young lion and the dragon shall your trample under feet.

14 Because he has set his love upon me, therefore will I deliver him: I will set him on high, because he has known my name.

15 He shall call upon me, and I will answer him: I will be with him in trouble; I will deliver him, and honor him.

16 With long life will I satisfy him, and show him my salvation.

Day 19

Psalms 92

It is a good thing to give thanks unto the LORD, and to sing praises unto your name, O most High:

2 To show forth your loving kindness in the morning, and your faithfulness every night,

3 Upon an instrument of ten strings, and upon the psaltery; upon the harp with a solemn sound.

4 For you, LORD, hast made me glad through your work: I will triumph in the works of your hands.

5 O LORD, how great are your works! and your thoughts are very deep.

6 A brutish man knows not; neither doth a fool understand this.

7 When the wicked spring as the grass, and when all the workers of iniquity do flourish; it is that they shall be destroyed forever:

8 But you, LORD, are most high forevermore.

9 For, lo, your enemies, O LORD, for, lo, your enemies shall perish; all the workers of iniquity shall be scattered.

10 But my horn shall you exalt like the horn of an unicorn: I shall be anointed with fresh oil.

Day 19

11 My eye also shall see my desire on my enemies, and my ears shall hear my desire of the wicked that rise up against me.

12 The righteous shall flourish like the palm tree: he shall grow like a cedar in Lebanon.

13 Those that be planted in the house of the LORD shall flourish in the courts of our GOD.

14 They shall still bring forth fruit in old age; they shall be fat and flourishing;

15 To show that the LORD is upright: he is my rock, and there is no
unrighteousness in him.

Psalms 93

The LORD reigns, he is clothed with majesty; the LORD is clothed with strength, wherewith he has girded himself: the world also is established, that it cannot be moved.

2 Your throne is established of old: you are from everlasting.

3 The floods have lifted up, O LORD, the floods have lifted up their voice; the floods lift up their waves.

4 The LORD on high is mightier than the noise of many waters, yous, than the mighty waves of the sea.

5 Your testimonies are very sure: holiness becomes your house, O LORD, forever.

Psalms 94

O LORD GOD, to whom vengeance belongs; O GOD, to whom vengeance belongs, show yourself.

2 Lift up yourself, you judge of the earth: render a reward to the proud.

3 LORD, how long shall the wicked, how long shall the wicked triumph?

4 How long shall they utter and speak hard things? and all the workers of iniquity boast themselves?

5 They break in pieces your people, O LORD, and afflict your heritage.

6 They slay the widow and the stranger, and murder the fatherless.

7 Yet they say, The LORD shall not see, neither shall the GOD of Jacob regard it.

8 Understand, you brutish among the people: and you fools, when will you be wise?

9 He that planted the ear, shall he not hear? he that formed the eyes, shall he not see?

Day 19

10 He that chastises the heathen, shall not he correct? he that teaches man knowledge, shall not he know?

11 The LORD knows the thoughts of man, that they are vanity.

12 Blessed is the man whom you chasten, O LORD, and teach him out of your law;

13 That you may give him rest from the days of adversity, until the pit be dug for the wicked.

14 For the LORD will not cast off his people, neither will he forsake his inheritance.

15 But judgment shall return unto righteousness: and all the upright in heart shall follow it.

16 Who will rise up for me against the evildoers? or who will stand up for me against the workers of iniquity?

17 Unless the LORD had been my help, my soul had almost dwelt in silence.

18 When I said, My foot slipped; your mercy, O LORD, held me up.

19 In the multitude of my thoughts within me your comforts delight my soul.

20 Shall the throne of iniquity have fellowship with you, which framed mischief by a law?

21 They gather themselves together against the soul of the righteous, and condemn the innocent blood.

22 But the LORD is my defense; and my GOD is the rock of my refuge.

23 And he shall bring upon them their own iniquity, and shall cut them off in their own wickedness; yes, the LORD our GOD shall cut them off.

Psalms 95

O come, let us sing unto the LORD: let us make a joyful noise to the rock of our salvation.

2 Let us come before his presence with thanksgiving, and make a joyful noise unto him with psalms.

3 For the LORD is a great GOD, and a great King above all GODs.

4 In his hand are the deep places of the earth: the strength of the hills is his also.

5 The sea is his, and he made it: and his hands formed the dry land.

Day 19

6 O come, let us worship and bow down: let us kneel before the LORD our maker.

7 For he is our GOD; and we are the people of his pasture, and the sheep of his hand. Today if you will hear his voice,

8 Harden not your heart, as in the provocation, and as in the day of temptation in the wilderness:

9 When your fathers tempted me, proved me, and saw my work.

`v10 Forty years long was I grieved with this generation, and said, It is a people that do err in their heart, and they have not known my ways:

11 Unto whom I swore in my wrath that they should not enter into my rest.

Proverbs 19

19 Better is the poor that walketh in his integrity, than he that is perverse in his lips, and is a fool.

2 Also, that the soul be without knowledge, it is not good; and he that hasteth with his feet sinneth.

3 The foolishness of man perverteth his way: and his heart fretteth against the Lord.

Day 19

4 Wealth maketh many friends; but the poor is separated from his neighbour.

5 A false witness shall not be unpunished, and he that speaketh lies shall not escape.

6 Many will intreat the favour of the prince: and every man is a friend to him that giveth gifts.

7 All the brethren of the poor do hate him: how much more do his friends go far from him? he pursueth them with words, yout they are wanting to him.

8 He that getteth wisdom loveth his own soul: he that keepeth understanding shall find good.

9 A false witness shall not be unpunished, and he that speaketh lies shall perish.

10 Delight is not seemly for a fool; much less for a servant to have rule over princes.

11 The discretion of a man deferreth his anger; and it is his glory to pass over a transgression.

12 The king's wrath is as the roaring of a lion; but his favour is as dew upon the grass.

13 A foolish son is the calamity of his father: and the contentions of a wife are a continual dropping.

Day 19

14 House and riches are the inheritance of fathers: and a prudent wife is from the Lord.

15 Slothfulness casteth into a deep sleep; and an idle soul shall suffer hunger.

16 He that keepeth the commandment keepeth his own soul; but he that despiseth his ways shall die.

17 He that has pity upon the poor lendeth unto the Lord; and that which he has given will he pay him again.

18 Chasten your son while there is hope, and let not your soul spare for his crying.

19 A man of great wrath shall suffer punishment: for if you deliver him, yout you must do it again.

20 Hear counsel, and receive instruction, that you mayoust be wise in your latter end.

21 There are many devices in a man's heart; nevertheless the counsel of the Lord, that shall stand.

22 The desire of a man is his kindness: and a poor man is better than a liar.

23 The fear of the Lord tendeth to life: and he that has it shall abide satisfied; he shall not be visited with evil.

24 A slothful man hideth his hand in his bosom, and will not so much as bring it to his mouth again.

25 Smite a scorner, and the simple will beware: and reprove one that has understanding, and he will understand knowledge.

26 He that wasteth his father, and chaseth away his mother, is a son that causeth shame, and bringeth reproach.

27 Cease, my son, to hear the instruction that causeth to err from the words of knowledge.

28 An ungodly witness scorneth judgment: and the mouth of the wicked devoureth iniquity.

29 Judgments are prepared for scorners, and stripes for the back of fools.

Day 19

Day 20

"Righteousness exalts a nation and will do the same for an individual, family or corporation." ~ Dr Will

Psalms 96

O sing unto the LORD a new song: sing unto the LORD, all the earth.

2 Sing unto the LORD, bless his name; show forth his salvation from day to day.

3 Declare his glory among the heathen, his wonders among all people.

4 For the LORD is great, and greatly to be praised: he is to be feared above all GODs.

5 For all the GODs of the nations are idols: but the LORD made the heavens.

6 Honor and majesty are before him: strength and beauty are in his sanctuary.

7 Give unto the LORD, O you kindred of the people, give unto the LORD glory and strength.

8 Give unto the LORD the glory due unto his name: bring an offering, and come into his courts.

9 O worship the LORD in the beauty of holiness: fear before him, all the earth.

10 Say among the heathen that the LORD reigns: the world also shall be established that it shall not be moved: he shall judge the people righteously.

11 Let the heavens rejoice, and let the earth be glad; let the sea roar, and the fullness thereof.

12 Let the field be joyful, and all that is therein: then shall all the trees of the wood rejoice

13 Before the LORD: for he comes, for he comes to judge the earth: he shall judge the world with righteousness, and the people with his truth.

Psalms 97

The LORD reigns; let the earth rejoice; let the multitude of isles be glad thereof.

2 Clouds and darkness are round about him: righteousness and judgment are the habitation of his throne.

3 A fire goes before him, and burns up his enemies round about.

Day 20

4 His lightning enlightened the world: the earth saw, and trembled.

5 The hills melted like wax at the presence of the LORD, at the presence of the Lord of the whole earth.

6 The heavens declare his righteousness, and all the people see his glory.

7 Confounded be all they that serve graven images, that boast themselves of idols: worship him, all you GODs.

8 Zion heard, and was glad; and the daughters of Judah rejoiced because of your judgments, O LORD.

9 For your, LORD, are high above all the earth: you are exalted far above all GODs.

10 You that love the LORD, hate evil: he preserves the souls of his saints; he delivers them out of the hand of the wicked.

11 Light is sown for the righteous, and gladness for the upright in heart.

12 Rejoice in the LORD, you righteous; and give thanks at the remembrance of his holiness.

Day 20

Psalms 98

O sing unto the LORD a new song; for he has done marvelous things: his right hand, and his holy arm, has gotten him the victory.

2 The LORD has made known his salvation: his righteousness has he openly showed in the sight of the heathen.

3 He has remembered his mercy and his truth toward the house of Israel: all the ends of the earth have seen the salvation of our GOD.

4 Make a joyful noise unto the LORD, all the earth: make a loud noise, and rejoice, and sing praise.

5 Sing unto the LORD with the harp; with the harp, and the voice of a psalm.

6 With trumpets and sound of cornet make a joyful noise before the LORD, the King.

7 Let the sea roar and the fullness thereof; the world and they that dwell therein.

8 Let the floods clap their hands: let the hills be joyful together

9 Before the LORD; for he comes to judge the earth: with righteousness shall he judge the world, and the people with equity.

Psalms 99

The LORD reigns; let the people tremble: he sits between the cherubims; let the earth be moved.

2 The LORD is great in Zion; and he is high above all the people.

3 Let them praise your great and terrible name; for it is holy.

4 The king's strength also loves judgment; you dost establish equity, you execute judgment and righteousness in Jacob.

5 Exalt you the LORD our GOD, and worship at his footstool; for he is holy.

6 Moses and Aaron among his priests, and Samuel among them that call upon his name; they called upon the LORD, and he answered them.

7 He spoke unto them in the cloudy pillar: they kept his testimonies, and the ordinance that he gave them.

Day 20

8 You answered them, O LORD our GOD: you was a GOD that forgave them, yough you took vengeance of their inventions.

9 Exalt the LORD our GOD, and worship at his holy hill; for the LORD our GOD is holy.

Psalms 100

Make a joyful noise unto the LORD, all you lands.

2 Serve the LORD with gladness: come before his presence with singing.

3 Know you that the LORD he is GOD: it is he that has made us, and not we ourselves; we are his people, and the sheep of his pasture.

4 Enter into his gates with thanksgiving, and into his courts with praise: be thankful unto him, and bless his name.

5 For the LORD is good; his mercy is everlasting; and his truth endures to all generations.

Proverbs 20

Wine is a mocker, strong drink is raging: and whosoever is deceived thereby is not wise.

2 The fear of a king is as the roaring of a lion: whoso provoketh him to anger sinneth against his own soul.

3 It is an honour for a man to cease from strife: but every fool will be meddling.

4 The sluggard will not plow by reason of the cold; therefore shall he beg in harvest, and have nothing.

5 Counsel in the heart of man is like deep water; but a man of understanding will draw it out.

6 Most men will proclaim every one his own goodness: but a faithful man who can find?

7 The just man walketh in his integrity: his children are blessed after him.

8 A king that sitteth in the throne of judgment scattereth away all evil with his eyes.

9 Who can say, I have made my heart clean, I am pure from my sin?

10 Divers weights, and divers measures, both of them are alike abomination to the Lord.

11 Even a child is known by his doings, whether his work be pure, and whether it be right.

12 The hearing ear, and the seeing eye, the Lord has made even both of them.

Day 20

13 Love not sleep, lest you come to poverty; open your eyes, and you shall be satisfied with bread.

14 It is naught, it is naught, saith the buyour: but when he is gone his way, then he boasteth.

15 There is gold, and a multitude of rubies: but the lips of knowledge are a precious jewel.

16 Take his garment that is surety for a stranger: and take a pledge of him for a strange woman.

17 Bread of deceit is sweet to a man; but afterwards his mouth shall be filled with gravel.

18 Every purpose is established by counsel: and with good advice make war.

19 He that goeth about as a talebearer revealeth secrets: therefore meddle not with him that flattereth with his lips.

20 Whoso curseth his father or his mother, his lamp shall be put out in obscure darkness.

21 An inheritance may be gotten hastily at the beginning; but the end thereof shall not be blessed.

22 Say not you, I will recompense evil; but wait on the Lord, and he shall save thee.

23 Divers weights are an abomination unto the Lord; and a false balance is not good.

24 Man's goings are of the Lord; how can a man then understand his own way?

25 It is a snare to the man who devoureth that which is holy, and after vows to make enquiry.

26 A wise king scattereth the wicked, and bringeth the wheel over them.

27 The spirit of man is the candle of the Lord, searching all the inward parts of the belly.

28 Mercy and truth preserve the king: and his throne is upholden by mercy.

29 The glory of young men is their strength: and the beauty of old men is the grey head.

30 The blueness of a wound cleanseth away evil: so do stripes the inward parts of the belly.

Day 20

Day 21

"The manner in which the average person lives is closely associated with what they see in and what they believe about themselves." ~ Dr Will

Psalms 101

I will sing of mercy and judgment: unto you, O LORD, will I sing.

2 I will behave myself wisely in a perfect way. O when will you come unto me? I will walk within my house with a perfect heart.

3 I will set no wicked thing before my eyes: I hate the work of them that turn aside; it shall not cleave to me.

4 A froward heart shall depart from me: I will not know a wicked person.

5 Whoso privily slanders his neighbor, him will I cut off: him that has a high look and a proud heart will not I suffer.

6 My eyes shall be upon the faithful of the land, that they may dwell with me: he that walk in a perfect way, he shall serve me.

Day 21

7 He that works deceit shall not dwell within my house: he that tells lies shall not tarry in my sight.

8 I will early destroy all the wicked of the land; that I may cut off all wicked doers from the city of the LORD.

Psalms 102

Hear my prayer, O LORD, and let my cry come unto you.

2 Hide not your face from me in the day when I am in trouble; incline your ear unto me: in the day when I call answer me speedily.

3 For my days are consumed like smoke, and my bones are burned as a hearth.

4 My heart is smitten, and withered like grass; so that I forget to eat my bread.

5 By reason of the voice of my groaning my bones cleave to my skin.

6 I am like a pelican of the wilderness: I am like an owl of the desert.

7 I watch, and am as a sparrow alone upon the house top.

8 My enemies reproach me all the day; and they that are mad against me are sworn against me.

9 For I have eaten ashes like bread, and mingled my drink with weeping,

10 Because of your indignation and your wrath: for you have lifted me up, and cast me down.

11 My days are like a shadow that declines; and I am withered like grass.

12 But you, O LORD, shall endure forever; and your remembrance unto all generations.

13 You shall arise, and have mercy upon Zion: for the time to favor her, yes, the set time, is come.

14 For your servants take pleasure in her stones, and favor the dust thereof.

15 So the heathen shall fear the name of the LORD, and all the kings of the earth your glory.

16 When the LORD shall build up Zion, he shall appear in his glory.

17 He will regard the prayer of the destitute, and not despise their prayer.

18 This shall be written for the generation to come: and the people which shall be created shall praise the LORD.

Day 21

19 For he has looked down from the height of his sanctuary; from heaven did the LORD behold the earth;

20 To hear the groaning of the prisoner; to loose those that are appointed to death;

21 To declare the name of the LORD in Zion, and his praise in Jerusalem;

22 When the people are gathered together, and the kingdoms, to serve the LORD.

23 He weakened my strength in the way; he shortened my days.

24 I said, O my GOD, take me not away in the midst of my days: your years are throughout all generations.

25 Of old hast your laid the foundation of the earth: and the heavens are the work of your hands.

26 They shall perish, but your shall endure: yes, all of them shall wax old like a garment; as a vesture shall you change them, and they shall be changed:

27 But you are the same, and your years shall have no end.

28 The children of your servants shall continue, and their seed shall be established before you.

Day 21

Psalms 103

Bless the LORD, O my soul: and all that is within me, bless his holy name.

2 Bless the LORD, O my soul, and forget not all his benefits:

3 Who forgives all your iniquities; who heals all your diseases;

4 Who redeems your life from destruction; who crowns you with loving kindness and tender mercies;

5 Who satisfies your mouth with good things; so that your youth is renewed like the eagle's.

6 The LORD executes righteousness and judgment for all that are oppressed.

7 He made known his ways unto Moses, his acts unto the children of Israel.

8 The LORD is merciful and gracious, slow to anger, and plenteous in mercy.

9 He will not always chide: neither will he keep his anger forever.

10 He has not dealt with us after our sins; nor rewarded us according to our iniquities.

Day 21

11 For as the heaven is high above the earth, so great is his mercy toward them that fear him.

12 As far as the east is from the west, so far has he removed our transgressions from us.

13 Like as a father pities his children, so the LORD pities them that fear him.

14 For he knows our frame; he remembers that we are dust.

15 As for man, his days are as grass: as a flower of the field, so he flourishes.

16 For the wind passes over it, and it is gone; and the place thereof shall know it no more.

17 But the mercy of the LORD is from everlasting to everlasting upon them that fear him, and his righteousness unto children's children;

18 To such as keep his covenant, and to those that remember his commandments to do them.

19 The LORD has prepared his throne in the heavens; and his kingdom rules over all.

20 Bless the LORD, you his angels, that excel in strength, that do his commandments, hearkening unto the voice of his word.

21 Bless you the LORD, all you his hosts; you ministers of his, that do his pleasure.

22 Bless the LORD, all his works in all places of his dominion: bless the LORD, O my soul.

Psalms 104

Bless the LORD, O my soul. O LORD my GOD, you are very great; you are clothed with honor and majesty.

2 Who covers yourself with light as with a garment: who stretches out the heavens like a curtain:

3 Who lays the beams of his chambers in the waters: who makes the clouds his chariot: who walks upon the wings of the wind:

4 Who makes his angels spirits; his ministers a flaming fire:

5 Who laid the foundations of the earth, that it should not be removed forever.

6 You covered it with the deep as with a garment: the waters stood above the mountains.

7 At your rebuke they fled; at the voice of your thunder they hasted away.

Day 21

8 They go up by the mountains; they go down by the valleys unto the place which you have founded for them.

9 You have set a bound that they may not pass over; that they turn not again to cover the earth.

10 He sends the springs into the valleys, which run among the hills.

11 They give drink to every beast of the field: the wild asses quench their thirst.

12 By them shall the fowls of the heaven have their habitation, which sing among the branches.

13 He waters the hills from his chambers: the earth is satisfied with the fruit of your works.

14 He causes the grass to grow for the cattle, and herb for the service of man: that he may bring forth food out of the earth;

15 And wine that makes glad the heart of man, and oil to make his face to shine, and bread which strengthens man's heart.

16 The trees of the LORD are full of sap; the cedars of Lebanon, which he has planted;

17 Where the birds make their nests: as for the stork, the fir trees are her house.

18 The high hills are a refuge for the wild goats; and the rocks for the conies.

19 He appointed the moon for seasons: the sun knows his going down.

20 You make darkness, and it is night: wherein all the beasts of the forest do creep forth.

21 The young lions roar after their prey, and seek their meat from GOD.

22 The sun arises, they gather themselves together, and lay them down in their dens.

23 Man goes forth unto his work and to his labor until the evening.

24 O LORD, how manifold are your works! in wisdom hast you made them all: the earth is full of your riches.

25 So is this great and wide sea, wherein are things creeping innumerable, both small and great beasts.

26 There go the ships: there is that leviathan, whom you have made to play therein.

27 These wait all upon you; that you may give them their meat in due season.

Day 21

28 That you give them they gather: your open your hand, they are filled with good.

29 You hide your face, they are troubled: you take away their breath, they die, and return to their dust.

30 You send forth your spirit, they are created: and you renew the face of the earth.

31 The glory of the LORD shall endure forever: the LORD shall rejoice in his works.

32 He looked on the earth, and it trembled: he touched the hills, and they smoke.

33 I will sing unto the LORD as long as I live: I will sing praise to my GOD while I have my being.

34 My meditation of him shall be sweet: I will be glad in the LORD.

35 Let the sinners be consumed out of the earth, and let the wicked be no more. Bless you the LORD, O my soul. Praise you the LORD.

ttt

O give thanks unto the LORD; call upon his name: make known his deeds among the people.

2 Sing unto him, sing psalms unto him: talk you of all his wondrous works.

3 Glory you in his holy name: let the heart of them rejoice that seek the LORD.

4 Seek the LORD, and his strength: seek his face evermore.

5 Remember his marvelous works that he has done; his wonders, and the judgments of his mouth;

6 O you seed of Abraham his servant, you children of Jacob his
chosen.

7 He is the LORD our GOD: his judgments are in all the earth.

8 He has remembered his covenant forever, the word which he commanded to a yousand generations.

9 Which covenant he made with Abraham, and his oath unto Isaac;

10 And confirmed the same unto Jacob for a law, and to Israel for an everlasting covenant:

11 Saying, Unto you will I give the land of Canaan, the lot of your inheritance:

Day 21

12 When they were but a few men in number; yous, very few, and strangers in it.

13 When they went from one nation to another, from one kingdom to another people;

14 He suffered no man to do them wrong: yous, he reproved kings for their sakes;

15 Saying, Touch not my anointed, and do my prophets no harm.

16 Moreover he called for a famine upon the land: he brake the
whole staff of bread.

17 He sent a man before them, even Joseph, who was sold for a servant:

18 Whose feet they hurt with fetters: he was laid in iron:

19 Until the time that his word came: the word of the LORD tried him.

20 The king sent and loosed him; even the ruler of the people, and
let him go free.

21 He made him lord of his house, and ruler of all his substance:

22 To bind his princes at his pleasure; and teach his senators wisdom.

23 Israel also came into Egypt; and Jacob sojourned in the land of Ham.

24 And he increased his people greatly; and made them stronger than their enemies.

25 He turned their heart to hate his people, to deal subtly with his servants.

26 He sent Moses his servant; and Aaron whom he had chosen.

27 They showed his signs among them, and wonders in the land of
Ham.

28 He sent darkness, and made it dark; and they rebelled not against his word.

29 He turned their waters into blood, and slew their fish.

30 Their land brought forth frogs in abundance, in the chambers of their kings.

31 He spoke, and there came divers sorts of flies, and lice in all their coasts.

32 He gave them hail for rain, and flaming fire in their land.

Day 21

33 He smote their vines also and their fig trees; and broke the trees of their coasts.

34 He spoke, and the locusts came, and caterpillars, and that without number,

35 And did eat up all the herbs in their land, and devoured the fruit of their ground.

36 He smote also all the firstborn in their land, the chief of all their strength.

37 He brought them forth also with silver and gold: and there was not one feeble person among their tribes.

38 Egypt was glad when they departed: for the fear of them fell upon them.

39 He spread a cloud for a covering; and fire to give light in the night.

40 The people asked, and he brought quails, and satisfied them with the bread of heaven.

41 He opened the rock, and the waters gushed out; they ran in the dry places like a river.

42 For he remembered his holy promise, and Abraham his servant.

43 And he brought forth his people with joy, and his chosen with gladness:

44 And gave them the lands of the heathen: and they inherited the labor of the people;

45 That they might observe his statutes, and keep his laws. Praise you the LORD.

Proverbs 21

The king's heart is in the hand of the Lord, as the rivers of water: he turneth it whithersoever he will.

2 Every way of a man is right in his own eyes: but the Lord pondereth the hearts.

3 To do justice and judgment is more acceptable to the Lord than sacrifice.

4 An high look, and a proud heart, and the plowing of the wicked, is sin.

5 The thoughts of the diligent tend only to plenteousness; but of every one that is hasty only to want.

6 The getting of treasures by a lying tongue is a vanity tossed to and fro of them that seek death.

7 The robbery of the wicked shall destroy them; because they refuse to do judgment.

Day 21

8 The way of man is froward and strange: but as for the pure, his work is right.

9 It is better to dwell in a corner of the housetop, than with a brawling woman in a wide house.

10 The soul of the wicked desireth evil: his neighbour findeth no favour in his eyes.

11 When the scorner is punished, the simple is made wise: and when the wise is instructed, he receiveth knowledge.

12 The righteous man wisely considereth the house of the wicked: but GOD overthroweth the wicked for their wickedness.

13 Whoso stoppeth his ears at the cry of the poor, he also shall cry himself, but shall not be heard.

14 A gift in secret pacifieth anger: and a reward in the bosom strong wrath.

15 It is joy to the just to do judgment: but destruction shall be to the workers of iniquity.

16 The man that wandereth out of the way of understanding shall remain in the congregation of the dead.

17 He that loveth pleasure shall be a poor man: he that loveth wine and oil shall not be rich.

Day 21

18 The wicked shall be a ransom for the righteous, and the transgressor for the upright.

19 It is better to dwell in the wilderness, than with a contentious and an angry woman.

20 There is treasure to be desired and oil in the dwelling of the wise; but a foolish man spendeth it up.

21 He that followeth after righteousness and mercy findeth life, righteousness, and honour.

22 A wise man scaleth the city of the mighty, and casteth down the strength of the confidence thereof.

23 Whoso keepeth his mouth and his tongue keepeth his soul from troubles.

24 Proud and haughty scorner is his name, who dealeth in proud wrath.

25 The desire of the slothful killeth him; for his hands refuse to labour.

26 He coveteth greedily all the day long: but the righteous giveth and spareth not.

27 The sacrifice of the wicked is abomination: how much more, when he bringeth it with a wicked mind?

Day 21

28 A false witness shall perish: but the man that heareth speaketh constantly.

29 A wicked man hardeneth his face: but as for the upright, he directeth his way.

30 There is no wisdom nor understanding nor counsel against the Lord.

31 The horse is prepared against the day of battle: but safety is of the Lord.

Day 22

"Out of chaos comes order but it is a higher degree of order that existed before the confusion." ~ Bob Proctor

Psalms 106

Praise you the LORD. O give thanks unto the LORD; for he is good: for his mercy endures forever.

2 Who can utter the mighty acts of the LORD? who can show forth all his praise?

3 Blessed are they that keep judgment, and he that doeth righteousness at all times.

4 Remember me, O LORD, with the favor that you bear unto your people: O visit me with your salvation;

5 That I may see the good of your chosen, that I may rejoice in the gladness of your nation, that I may glory with your inheritance.

6 We have sinned with our fathers, we have committed iniquity, we have done wickedly.

7 Our fathers understood not your wonders in Egypt; they remembered not the multitude of your mercies; but provoked him at the sea, even at the Red sea.

Day 22

8 Nevertheless he saved them for his name's sake, that he might make his mighty power to be known.

9 He rebuked the Red sea also, and it was dried up: so he led them through the depths, as through the wilderness.

10 And he saved them from the hand of him that hated them, and redeemed them from the hand of the enemy.

11 And the waters covered their enemies: there was not one of them left.

12 Then believed they his words; they sang his praise.

13 They soon forgot his works; they waited not for his counsel:

14 But lusted exceedingly in the wilderness, and tempted GOD in the desert.

15 And he gave them their request; but sent leanness into their soul.

16 They envied Moses also in the camp, and Aaron the saint of the LORD.

17 The earth opened and swallowed up Dathan, and covered the company of Abiram.

18 And a fire was kindled in their company; the flame burned up the wicked.

Day 22

19 They made a calf in Horeb, and worshipped the molten image.

20 Thus they changed their glory into the similitude of an ox that eats grass.

21 They forgot GOD their Savior, which had done great things in Egypt;

22 Wondrous works in the land of Ham, and terrible things by the Red sea.

23 Therefore he said that he would destroy them, had not Moses his chosen stood before him in the breach, to turn away his wrath, lest he should destroy them.

24 Yes, they despised the pleasant land, they believed not his word:

25 But murmured in their tents, and hearkened not unto the voice of the LORD.

26 Therefore he lifted up his hand against them, to overthrow them in the wilderness:

27 To overthrow their seed also among the nations, and to scatter them in the lands.

28 They joined themselves also unto Baalpeor, and ate the sacrifices of the dead.

Day 22

29 Thus they provoked him to anger with their inventions: and the plague brake in upon them.

30 Then stood up Phinehas, and executed judgment: and so the plague was stayed.

31 And that was counted unto him for righteousness unto all generations forevermore.

32 They angered him also at the waters of strife, so that it went ill with Moses for their sakes:

33 Because they provoked his spirit, so that he spoke unadvisedly with his lips.

34 They did not destroy the nations, concerning whom the LORD commanded them:

35 But were mingled among the heathen, and learned their works.

36 And they served their idols: which were a snare unto them.

37 Yes, they sacrificed their sons and their daughters unto devils,

38 And shed innocent blood, even the blood of their sons and of their daughters, whom they sacrificed unto the idols of Canaan: and the land was polluted with blood.

39 Thus were they defiled with their own works, and went a whoring with their own inventions.

40 Therefore was the wrath of the LORD kindled against his people, insomuch that he abhorred his own inheritance.

41 And he gave them into the hand of the heathen; and they that hated them ruled over them.

42 Their enemies also oppressed them, and they were brought into subjection under their hand.

43 Many times did he deliver them; but they provoked him with their counsel, and were brought low for their iniquity.

44 Nevertheless he regarded their affliction, when he heard their cry:

45 And he remembered for them his covenant, and repented according to the multitude of his mercies.

46 He made them also to be pitied of all those that carried them captives.

47 Save us, O LORD our GOD, and gather us from among the heathen, to give thanks unto your holy name, and to triumph in your praise.

48 Blessed be the Lord GOD of Israel from everlasting to everlasting: and let all the people say, Amen. Praise you the LORD.

Day 22

Psalms 107

O give thanks unto the LORD, for he is good: for his mercy endures forever.

2 Let the redeemed of the LORD say so, whom he has redeemed from the hand of the enemy;

3 And gathered them out of the lands, from the east, and from the west, from the north, and from the south.

4 They wandered in the wilderness in a solitary way; they found no city to dwell in.

5 Hungry and thirsty, their soul fainted in them.

6 Then they cried unto the LORD in their trouble, and he delivered them out of their distresses.

7 And he led them forth by the right way, that they might go to a city of habitation.

8 Oh that men would praise the LORD for his goodness, and for his wonderful works to the children of men!

9 For he satisfies the longing soul, and fills the hungry soul with goodness.

10 Such as sit in darkness and in the shadow of death, being bound in affliction and iron;

11 Because they rebelled against the words of GOD, and contemned the counsel of the most High:

12 Therefore he brought down their heart with labor; they fell down, and there was none to help.

13 Then they cried unto the LORD in their trouble, and he saved them out of their distresses.

14 He brought them out of darkness and the shadow of death, and broke their bands in sunder.

15 Oh that men would praise the LORD for his goodness, and for his wonderful works to the children of men!

16 For he has broken the gates of brass, and cut the bars of iron in sunder.

17 Fools because of their transgression, and because of their iniquities, are afflicted.

18 Their soul abhor all manner of meat; and they draw near unto the gates of death.

19 Then they cry unto the LORD in their trouble, and he saves them out of their distresses.

20 He sent his word, and healed them, and delivered them from their destructions.

Day 22

21 Oh that men would praise the LORD for his goodness, and for his wonderful works to the children of men!

22 And let them sacrifice the sacrifices of thanksgiving, and declare his works with rejoicing.

23 They that go down to the sea in ships, that do business in great waters;

24 These see the works of the LORD, and his wonders in the deep.

25 For he commanded, and raised the stormy wind, which lifted up the waves thereof.

26 They mount up to the heaven, they go down again to the depths: their soul is melted because of trouble.

27 They reel to and fro, and stagger like a drunken man, and are at their wits' end.

28 Then they cry unto the LORD in their trouble, and he brings them out of their distresses.

29 He makes the storm a calm, so that the waves thereof are still.

30 Then are they glad because they be quiet; so he brings them unto their desired haven.

31 Oh that men would praise the LORD for his goodness, and for his wonderful works to the children of men!

32 Let them exalt him also in the congregation of the people, and praise him in the assembly of the elders.

33 He turned rivers into a wilderness, and the water springs into dry ground;

34 A fruitful land into barrenness, for the wickedness of them that dwell therein.

35 He turned the wilderness into a standing water, and dry ground into water springs.

36 And there he makes the hungry to dwell, that they may prepare a city for habitation;

37 And sow the fields, and plant vineyards, which may yield fruits of increase.

38 He blessed them also, so that they are multiplied greatly; and suffered not their cattle to decrease.

39 Again, they are diminished and brought low through oppression, affliction, and sorrow.

40 He poured contempt upon princes, and causes them to wander in the wilderness, where there is no way.

Day 22

41 Yet sets he the poor on high from affliction, and makes him families like a flock.

42 The righteous shall see it, and rejoice: and all iniquity shall stop her mouth.

43 Whoso is wise, and will observe these things, even they shall understand the loving kindness of the LORD.

Psalms 108

O GOD, my heart is fixed; I will sing and give praise, even with my glory.

2 Awake, psaltery and harp: I myself will awake early.

3 I will praise you, O LORD, among the people: and I will sing praises unto you among the nations.

4 For your mercy is great above the heavens: and your truth reaches unto the clouds.

5 Be your exalted, O GOD, above the heavens: and your glory above all the earth;

6 That your beloved may be delivered: save with your right hand, and answer me.

7 GOD has spoken in his holiness; I will rejoice, I will divide Shechem, and mete out the valley of Succoth.

8 Gilead is my; Manasseh is my; Ephraim also is the strength of my head; Judah is my lawgiver;

9 Moab is my wash pot; over Edom will I cast out my shoe; over Philistia will I triumph.

10 Who will bring me into the strong city? who will lead me into Edom?

11 Will not your, O GOD, who hast cast us off? and will not you, O GOD, go forth with our hosts?

12 Give us help from trouble: for vain is the help of man.

13 Through GOD we shall do valiantly: for he it is that shall tread down our enemies.

Psalms 109

Hold not your peace, O GOD of my praise;

2 For the mouth of the wicked and the mouth of the deceitful are opened against me: they have spoken against me with a lying tongue.

3 They compassed me about also with words of hatred; and fought against me without a cause.

4 For my love they are my adversaries: but I give myself unto prayer.

Day 22

5 And they have rewarded me evil for good, and hatred for my love.

6 Set you a wicked man over him: and let Satan stand at his right hand.

7 When he shall be judged, let him be condemned: and let his prayer become sin.

8 Let his days be few; and let another take his office.

9 Let his children be fatherless, and his wife a widow.

10 Let his children be continually vagabonds, and beg: let them seek their bread also out of their desolate places.

11 Let the extortioner catch all that he has; and let the strangers spoil his labor.

12 Let there be none to extend mercy unto him: neither let there be any to favor his fatherless children.

13 Let his posterity be cut off; and in the generation following let their name be blotted out.

14 Let the iniquity of his fathers be remembered with the LORD;
and let not the sin of his mother be blotted out.

15 Let them be before the LORD continually, that he may cut off the memory of them from the earth.

16 Because that he remembered not to show mercy, but persecuted the poor and needy man, that he might even slay the broken in heart.

17 As he loved cursing, so let it come unto him: as he delighted not in blessing, so let it be far from him.

18 As he clothed himself with cursing like as with his garment, so let it come into his bowels like water, and like oil into his bones.

19 Let it be unto him as the garment which covers him, and for a girdle wherewith he is girded continually.

20 Let this be the reward of my adversaries from the LORD, and of them that speak evil against my soul.

21 But do you for me, O GOD the Lord, for your name's sake: because your mercy is good, deliver you me.

22 For I am poor and needy, and my heart is wounded within me.

23 I am gone like the shadow when it declines: I am tossed up and down as the locust.

24 My knees are weak through fasting; and my flesh failed of fatness.

25 I became also a reproach unto them: when they looked upon me they shake their heads.

Day 22

26 Help me, O LORD my GOD: O save me according to your mercy:

27 That they may know that this is your hand; that you, LORD, hast done it.

28 Let them curse, but bless you: when they arise, let them be ashamed; but let your servant rejoice.

29 Let my adversaries be clothed with shame, and let them cover themselves with their own confusion, as with a mantle.

30 I will greatly praise the LORD with my mouth; yous, I will praise him among the multitude.

31 For he shall stand at the right hand of the poor, to save him from those that condemn his soul.

Psalms 110

The LORD said unto my Lord, Sit you at my right hand, until I make your enemies your footstool.

2 The LORD shall send the rod of your strength out of Zion: rule you in the midst of your enemies.

3 Your people shall be willing in the day of your power, in the beauties of holiness from the womb of the morning: you have the dew of your youth.

4 The LORD has sworn, and will not repent, You are a priest forever after the order of Melchizedek.

5 The Lord at your right hand shall strike through kings in the day of his wrath.

6 He shall judge among the heathen, he shall fill the places with the dead bodies; he shall wound the heads over many countries.

7 He shall drink of the brook in the way: therefore shall he lift up the head.

Proverbs 22

A good name is rather to be chosen than great riches, and loving favour rather than silver and gold.

2 The rich and poor meet together: the Lord is the maker of them all.

3 A prudent man foreseeth the evil, and hideth himself: but the simple pass on, and are punished.

4 By humility and the fear of the Lord are riches, and honour, and life.

5 Thorns and snares are in the way of the froward: he that doth keep his soul shall be far from them.

Day 22

6 Train up a child in the way he should go: and when he is old, he will not depart from it.

7 The rich ruleth over the poor, and the borrower is servant to the lender.

8 He that soweth iniquity shall reap vanity: and the rod of his anger shall fail.

9 He that has a bountiful eye shall be blessed; for he giveth of his bread to the poor.

10 Cast out the scorner, and contention shall go out; yea, strife and reproach shall cease.

11 He that loveth pureness of heart, for the grace of his lips the king shall be his friend.

12 The eyes of the Lord preserve knowledge, and he overthroweth the words of the transgressor.

13 The slothful man saith, There is a lion without, I shall be slain in the streets.

14 The mouth of strange women is a deep pit: he that is abhorred of the Lord shall fall therein.

15 Foolishness is bound in the heart of a child; but the rod of correction shall drive it far from him.

16 He that oppresseth the poor to increase his riches, and he that giveth to the rich, shall surely come to want.

17 Bow down your ear, and hear the words of the wise, and apply your heart unto my knowledge.

18 For it is a pleasant thing if you keep them within thee; they shall withal be fitted in your lips.

19 That your trust may be in the Lord, I have made known to thee this day, even to thee.

20 Have not I written to thee excellent things in counsels and knowledge,

21 That I might make thee know the certainty of the words of truth; that you mightest answer the words of truth to them that send unto thee?

22 Rob not the poor, because he is poor: neither oppress the afflicted in the gate:

23 For the Lord will plead their cause, and spoil the soul of those that spoiled them.

24 Make no friendship with an angry man; and with a furious man you shall not go:

25 Lest you learn his ways, and get a snare to your soul.

Day 22

26 Be not you one of them that strike hands, or of them that are sureties for debts.

27 If you hast nothing to pay, why should he take away your bed from under thee?

28 Remove not the ancient landmark, which your fathers have set.

29 Seest you a man diligent in his business? he shall stand before kings; he shall not stand before mean men.

Day 23

"A candle does not lose anything when it lights another candle it only spreads more light." ~Dr Will

Psalms 111

Praise you the LORD. I will praise the LORD with my whole heart, in the assembly of the upright, and in the congregation.

2 The works of the LORD are great, sought out of all them that have pleasure therein.

3 His work is honorable and glorious: and his righteousness endures forever.

4 He has made his wonderful works to be remembered: the LORD is gracious and full of compassion.

5 He has given meat unto them that fear him: he will ever be mindful of his covenant.

6 He has showed his people the power of his works, that he may give them the heritage of the heathen.

7 The works of his hands are verity and judgment; all his commandments are sure.

Day 23

8 They stand fast forever and ever, and are done in truth and uprightness.

9 He sent redemption unto his people: he has commanded his covenant forever: holy and reverend is his name.

10 The fear of the LORD is the beginning of wisdom: a good understanding have all they that do his commandments: his praise endures forever.

Psalms 112

Praise you the LORD. Blessed is the man that fears the LORD, that delights greatly in his commandments.

2 His seed shall be mighty upon earth: the generation of the upright shall be blessed.

3 Wealth and riches shall be in his house: and his righteousness endures forever.

4 Unto the upright there arises light in the darkness: he is gracious, and full of compassion, and righteous.

5 A good man shows favor, and lends: he will guide his affairs with discretion.

6 Surely he shall not be moved forever: the righteous shall be in everlasting remembrance.

7 He shall not be afraid of evil tidings: his heart is fixed, trusting in the LORD.

8 His heart is established, he shall not be afraid, until he see his desire upon his enemies.

9 He has dispersed, he has given to the poor; his righteousness endures forever; his horn shall be exalted with honor.

10 The wicked shall see it, and be grieved; he shall gnash with his teeth, and melt away: the desire of the wicked shall perish.

Psalms 113

Praise you the LORD. Praise, O you servants of the LORD, praise the name of the LORD.

2 Blessed be the name of the LORD from this time forth and forevermore.

3 From the rising of the sun unto the going down of the same the LORD's name is to be praised.

4 The LORD is high above all nations, and his glory above the heavens.

5 Who is like unto the LORD our GOD, who dwells on high,

6 Who humbles himself to behold the things that are in heaven, and in the earth!

7 He raises up the poor out of the dust, and lifts the needy out of the dunghill;

8 That he may set him with princes, even with the princes of his people.

9 He makes the barren woman to keep house, and to be a joyful mother of children. Praise you the LORD.

Psalms 114

When Israel went out of Egypt, the house of Jacob from a people of strange language;

2 Judah was his sanctuary, and Israel his dominion.

3 The sea saw it, and fled: Jordan was driven back.

4 The mountains skipped like rams, and the little hills like lambs.

5 What ailed you, O you sea, that you fled? you Jordan, that you was driven back?

6 You mountains, that you skipped like rams; and you little hills, like lambs?

7 Tremble, you earth, at the presence of the Lord, at the presence of the GOD of Jacob;

8 Which turned the rock into a standing water, the flint into a fountain of waters.

Psalms 115

Not unto us, O LORD, not unto us, but unto your name give glory, for your mercy, and for your truth's sake.

2 Wherefore should the heathen say, Where is now their GOD?

3 But our GOD is in the heavens: he has done whatsoever he has pleased.

4 Their idols are silver and gold, the work of men's hands.

5 They have mouths, but they speak not: eyes have they, but they see not:

6 They have ears, but they hear not: noses have they, but they smell not:

7 They have hands, but they handle not: feet have they, but they walk not: neither speak they through their throat.

8 They that make them are like unto them; so is every one that trusted in them.

Day 23

9 O Israel, trust you in the LORD: he is their help and their shield.

10 O house of Aaron, trust in the LORD: he is their help and their shield.

11 You that fear the LORD, trust in the LORD: he is their help and their shield.

12 The LORD has been mindful of us: he will bless us; he will bless the house of Israel; he will bless the house of Aaron.

13 He will bless them that fear the LORD, both small and great.

14 The LORD shall increase you more and more, you and your children.

15 You are blessed of the LORD which made heaven and earth.

16 The heaven, even the heavens, are the LORD's: but the earth has he given to the children of men.

17 The dead praise not the LORD, neither any that go down into silence.

18 But we will bless the LORD from this time forth and forevermore. Praise the LORD.

Proverbs 23

When you sittest to eat with a ruler, consider diligently what is before thee:

2 And put a knife to your throat, if you be a man given to appetite.

3 Be not desirous of his dainties: for they are deceitful meat.

4 Labour not to be rich: cease from your own wisdom.

5 Wilt you set your eyes upon that which is not? for riches certainly make themselves wings; they fly away as an eagle toward heaven.

6 Eat you not the bread of him that has an evil eye, neither desire you his dainty meats:

7 For as he thinketh in his heart, so is he: Eat and drink, saith he to thee; but his heart is not with thee.

8 The morsel which you hast eaten shall you vomit up, and lose your sweet words.

9 Speak not in the ears of a fool: for he will despise the wisdom of your words.

10 Remove not the old landmark; and enter not into the fields of the fatherless:

Day 23

11 For their redeemer is mighty; he shall plead their cause with thee.

12 Apply your heart unto instruction, and your ears to the words of knowledge.

13 Withhold not correction from the child: for if you beatest him with the rod, he shall not die.

14 You shall beat him with the rod, and shall deliver his soul from hell.

15 My son, if your heart be wise, my heart shall rejoice, even mine.

16 Yea, my reins shall rejoice, when your lips speak right things.

17 Let not your heart envy sinners: but be you in the fear of the Lord all the day long.

18 For surely there is an end; and your expectation shall not be cut off.

19 Hear you, my son, and be wise, and guide your heart in the way.

20 Be not among winebibbers; among riotous eaters of flesh:

Day 23

21 For the drunkard and the glutton shall come to poverty: and drowsiness shall clothe a man with rags.

22 Hearken unto your father that begat thee, and despise not your mother when she is old.

23 Buy the truth, and sell it not; also wisdom, and instruction, and understanding.

24 The father of the righteous shall greatly rejoice: and he that begetteth a wise child shall have joy of him.

25 Your father and your mother shall be glad, and she that bare thee shall rejoice.

26 My son, give me your heart, and let your eyes observe my ways.

27 For a whore is a deep ditch; and a strange woman is a narrow pit.

28 She also lieth in wait as for a prey, and increaseth the transgressors among men.

29 Who has woe? who has sorrow? who has contentions? who has babbling? who has wounds without cause? who has redness of eyes?

30 They that tarry long at the wine; they that go to seek mixed wine.

Day 23

31 Look not you upon the wine when it is red, when it giveth his colour in the cup, when it moveth itself aright.

32 At the last it biteth like a serpent, and stingeth like an adder.

33 Your eyes shall behold strange women, and your heart shall utter perverse things.

34 Yea, you shall be as he that lieth down in the midst of the sea, or as he that lieth upon the top of a mast.

35 They have stricken me, shall you say, and I was not sick; they have beaten me, and I felt it not: when shall I awake? I will seek it yout again.

Day 24

"One person with a commitment is worth more than 100 with an interest." ~Dr Will

Psalms 116

I love the LORD, because he has heard my voice and my supplications.

2 Because he has inclined his ear unto me, therefore will I call upon him as long as I live.

3 The sorrows of death compassed me, and the pains of hell gat hold upon me: I found trouble and sorrow.

4 Then called I upon the name of the LORD; O LORD, I beseech you, deliver my soul.

5 Gracious is the LORD, and righteous; yous, our GOD is merciful.

6 The LORD preserves the simple: I was brought low, and he helped me.

7 Return unto your rest, O my soul; for the LORD has dealt bountifully with you.

Day 24

8 For you have delivered my soul from death, my eyes from tears, and my feet from falling.

9 I will walk before the LORD in the land of the living.

10 I believed, therefore have I spoken: I was greatly afflicted:

11 I said in my haste, All men are liars.

12 What shall I render unto the LORD for all his benefits toward me?

13 I will take the cup of salvation, and call upon the name of the LORD.

14 I will pay my vows unto the LORD now in the presence of all his people.

15 Precious in the sight of the LORD is the death of his saints.

16 O LORD, truly I am your servant; I am your servant, and the son of your handmaid: you have loosed my bonds.

17 I will offer to you the sacrifice of thanksgiving, and will call upon the name of the LORD.

18 I will pay my vows unto the LORD now in the presence of all his people,

Day 24

19 In the courts of the LORD's house, in the midst of you, O Jerusalem. Praise you the LORD.

Psalms 117

O praise the LORD, all you nations: praise him, all you people.

2 For his merciful kindness is great toward us: and the truth of the LORD endureth forever. Praise you the LORD.

Psalms 118

O give thanks unto the LORD; for he is good: because his mercy endures forever.

2 Let Israel now say, that his mercy endures forever.

3 Let the house of Aaron now say, that his mercy endures forever.

4 Let them now that fear the LORD say, that his mercy endures forever.

5 I called upon the LORD in distress: the LORD answered me, and set me in a large place.

6 The LORD is on my side; I will not fear: what can man do unto me?

7 The LORD takes my part with them that help me: therefore shall I see my desire upon them that hate me.

8 It is better to trust in the LORD than to put confidence in man.

9 It is better to trust in the LORD than to put confidence in princes.

10 All nations compassed me about: but in the name of the LORD will I destroy them.

11 They compassed me about; yous, they compassed me about: but in the name of the LORD I will destroy them.

12 They compassed me about like bees; they are quenched as the fire of thorns: for in the name of the LORD I will destroy them.

13 You have thrust sore at me that I might fall: but the LORD helped me.

14 The LORD is my strength and song, and is become my salvation.

15 The voice of rejoicing and salvation is in the tabernacles of the righteous: the right hand of the LORD doeth valiantly.

16 The right hand of the LORD is exalted: the right hand of the LORD does valiantly.

Day 24

17 I shall not die, but live, and declare the works of the LORD.

18 The LORD has chastened me sore: but he has not given me over unto death.

19 Open to me the gates of righteousness: I will go into them, and I will praise the LORD:

20 This gate of the LORD, into which the righteous shall enter.

21 I will praise you: for you have heard me, and are become my salvation.

22 The stone which the builders refused is become the head stone of the corner.

23 This is the LORD's doing; it is marvelous in our eyes.

24 This is the day which the LORD has made; we will rejoice and be glad in it.

25 Save now, I beseech you, O LORD: O LORD, I beseech you, send now prosperity.

26 Blessed be he that cometh in the name of the LORD: we have blessed you out of the house of the LORD.

27 GOD is the LORD, which has showed us light: bind the sacrifice with cords, even unto the horns of the altar.

Day 24

28 You are my GOD, and I will praise you: you are my GOD, I will exalt you.

29 O give thanks unto the LORD; for he is good: for his mercy endures forever.

Psalms 119 (Part 1)

Blessed are the undefiled in the way, who walk in the law of the LORD.

2 Blessed are they that keep his testimonies, and that seek him with the whole heart.

3 They also do no iniquity: they walk in his ways.

4 You have commanded us to keep your precepts diligently.

5 O that my ways were directed to keep your statutes!

6 Then shall I not be ashamed, when I have respect unto all your commandments.

7 I will praise you with uprightness of heart, when I shall have learned your righteous judgments.

8 I will keep your statutes: O forsake me not utterly.

9 Wherewithal shall a young man cleanse his way? by taking heed thereto according to your word.

10 With my whole heart have I sought you: O let me not wander from your commandments.

11 Your word have I hid in my heart, that I might not sin against you.

12 Blessed are you, O LORD: teach me your statutes.

13 With my lips have I declared all the judgments of your mouth.

14 I have rejoiced in the way of your testimonies, as much as in all riches.

15 I will meditate in your precepts, and have respect unto your ways.

16 I will delight myself in your statutes: I will not forget your word.

17 Deal bountifully with your servant, that I may live, and keep your word.

18 Open you my eyes, that I may behold wondrous things out of your law.

19 I am a stranger in the earth: hide not your commandments from me.

20 My soul breaks for the longing that it has unto your judgments at all times.

Day 24

21 You have rebuked the proud that are cursed, which do err from your commandments.

22 Remove from me reproach and contempt; for I have kept your testimonies.

23 Princes also did sit and speak against me: but your servant did meditate in your statutes.

24 Your testimonies also are my delight and my counselors.

25 My soul cleaves unto the dust: quicken you me according to your word.

26 I have declared my ways, and you heard me: teach me your statutes.

27 Make me to understand the way of your precepts: so shall I talk of your wondrous works.

28 My soul melts for heaviness: strengthen you me according unto your word.

29 Remove from me the way of lying: and grant me your law graciously.

30 I have chosen the way of truth: your judgments have I laid before me.

31 I have stuck unto your testimonies: O LORD, put me not to shame.

Day 24

32 I will run the way of your commandments, when you shall enlarge my heart.

33 Teach me, O LORD, the way of your statutes; and I shall keep it unto the end.

34 Give me understanding, and I shall keep your law; yous, I shall observe it with my whole heart.

35 Make me to go in the path of your commandments; for therein do I delight.

36 Incline my heart unto your testimonies, and not to covetousness.

37 Turn away my eyes from beholding vanity; and quicken you me in your way.

38 Establish your word unto your servant, who is devoted to your fear.

39 Turn away my reproach which I fear: for your judgments are good.

40 Behold, I have longed after your precepts: quicken me in your righteousness.

41 Let your mercies come also unto me, O LORD, even your salvation, according to your word.

42 So shall I have wherewith to answer him that reproached me: for I trust in your word.

43 And take not the word of truth utterly out of my mouth; for I have hoped in your judgments.

44 So shall I keep your law continually forever and ever.

45 And I will walk at liberty: for I seek your precepts.

46 I will speak of your testimonies also before kings, and will not be ashamed.

47 And I will delight myself in your commandments, which I have loved.

48 My hands also will I lift up unto your commandments, which I have loved; and I will meditate in your statutes.

49 Remember the word unto your servant, upon which you have caused me to hope.

50 This is my comfort in my affliction: for your word has quickened me.

51 The proud have had me greatly in derision: yet have I not declined from your law.

52 I remembered your judgments of old, O LORD; and have comforted myself.

53 Horror has taken hold upon me because of the wicked that forsake your law.

54 Your statutes have been my songs in the house of my pilgrimage.

55 I have remembered your name, O LORD, in the night, and have kept your law.

56 This I had, because I kept your precepts.

57 You are my portion, O LORD: I have said that I would keep your words.

58 I entreated your favor with my whole heart: be merciful unto me according to your word.

59 I thought on my ways, and turned my feet unto your testimonies.

60 I made haste, and delayed not to keep your commandments.

61 The bands of the wicked have robbed me: but I have not forgotten your law.

62 At midnight I will rise to give thanks unto you because of your righteous judgments.

63 I am a companion of all them that fear you, and of them that keep your precepts.

Day 24

64 The earth, O LORD, is full of your mercy: teach me your statutes.

65 You have dealt well with your servant, O LORD, according unto your word.

66 Teach me good judgment and knowledge: for I have believed your commandments.

67 Before I was afflicted I went astray: but now have I kept your word.

68 You are good, and do good; teach me your statutes.

69 The proud have forged a lie against me: but I will keep your precepts with my whole heart.

70 Their heart is as fat as grease; but I delight in your law.

71 It is good for me that I have been afflicted; that I might learn your statutes.

72 The law of your mouth is better unto me than thousands of gold and silver.

73 Your hands have made me and fashioned me: give me understanding, that I may learn your commandments.

74 They that fear you will be glad when they see me; because I have hoped in your word.

Day 24

75 I know, O LORD, that your judgments are right, and that you in faithfulness have afflicted me.

76 Let, I pray you, your merciful kindness be for my comfort, according to your word unto your servant.

77 Let your tender mercies come unto me, that I may live: for your law is my delight.

78 Let the proud be ashamed; for they dealt perversely with me without a cause: but I will meditate in your precepts.

79 Let those that fear you turn unto me, and those that have known your testimonies.

80 Let my heart be sound in your statutes; that I be not ashamed.

81 My soul fainted for your salvation: but I hope in your word.

82 My eyes fail for your word, saying, When will your comfort me?

83 For I am become like a bottle in the smoke; yet do I not forget your statutes.

84 How many are the days of your servant? when will your execute judgment on them that persecute me?

Day 24

85 The proud have dug pits for me, which are not after your law.

86 All your commandments are faithful: they persecute me wrongfully; help your me.

87 They had almost consumed me upon earth; but I forsook not your precepts.

88 Quicken me after your loving kindness; so shall I keep the testimony of your mouth.

Psalms 119 (Part 2)

Forever, O LORD, your word is settled in heaven.

90 Your faithfulness is unto all generations: you have established the earth, and it abides.

91 They continue this day according to your ordinances: for all are your servants.

92 Unless your law had been my delights, I should then have perished in my affliction.

93 I will never forget your precepts: for with them you have quickened me.

94 I am yours, save me; for I have sought your precepts.

Day 24

95 The wicked have waited for me to destroy me: but I will consider your testimonies.

96 I have seen an end of all perfection: but your commandment is exceeding broad.

97 O how love I your law! it is my meditation all the day.

98 Your through your commandments hast made me wiser than my enemies: for they are ever with me.

99 I have more understanding than all my teachers: for your testimonies are my meditation.

100 I understand more than the ancients, because I keep your precepts.

101 I have refrained my feet from every evil way, that I might keep your word.

102 I have not departed from your judgments: for you have taught me.

103 How sweet are your words unto my taste! yes, sweeter than honey to my mouth!

104 Through your precepts I get understanding: therefore I hate every false way.

105 Your word is a lamp unto my feet, and a light unto my path.

Day 24

106 I have sworn, and I will perform it, that I will keep your righteous judgments.

107 I am afflicted very much: quicken me, O LORD, according unto your word.

108 Accept, I beseech you, the freewill offerings of my mouth, O LORD, and teach me your judgments.

109 My soul is continually in my hand: yet do I not forget your law.

110 The wicked have laid a snare for me: yet I erred not from your precepts.

111 Your testimonies have I taken as a heritage forever: for they are the rejoicing of my heart.

112 I have inclined my heart to perform your statutes always, even unto the end.

113 I hate vain thoughts: but your law do I love.

114 You are my hiding place and my shield: I hope in your word.

115 Depart from me, you evildoers: for I will keep the commandments of my GOD.

116 Uphold me according unto your word, that I may live: and let me not be ashamed of my hope.

117 Hold you me up, and I shall be safe: and I will have respect unto your statutes continually.

118 You have trodden down all them that err from your statutes: for their deceit is falsehood.

119 You put away all the wicked of the earth like dross: therefore I love your testimonies.

120 My flesh trembles for fear of you; and I am afraid of your judgments.

121 I have done judgment and justice: leave me not to my oppressors.

122 Be surety for your servant for good: let not the proud oppress me.

123 My eyes fail for your salvation, and for the word of your righteousness.

124 Deal with your servant according unto your mercy, and teach me your statutes.

125 I am your servant; give me understanding, that I may know your testimonies.

126 It is time for you, LORD, to work: for they have made void your law.

Day 24

127 Therefore I love your commandments above gold; yes, above fine gold.

128 Therefore I esteem all your precepts concerning all things to be right; and I hate every false way.

129 Your testimonies are wonderful: therefore doth my soul keep them.

130 The entrance of your words gives light; it gives understanding unto the simple.

131 I opened my mouth, and panted: for I longed for your commandments.

132 Look your upon me, and be merciful unto me, as you used to do unto those that love your name.

133 Order my steps in your word: and let not any iniquity have dominion over me.

134 Deliver me from the oppression of man: so will I keep your precepts.

135 Make your face to shine upon your servant; and teach me your statutes.

136 Rivers of waters run down my eyes, because they keep not your law.

Day 24

137 Righteous are you, O LORD, and upright are your judgments.

138 Your testimonies that you have commanded are righteous and very faithful.

139 My zeal has consumed me, because my enemies have forgotten your words.

140 Your word is very pure: therefore your servant loves it.

141 I am small and despised: yet do not I forget your precepts.

142 Your righteousness is an everlasting righteousness, and your law is the truth.

143 Trouble and anguish have taken hold on me: yet your commandments are my delights.

144 The righteousness of your testimonies is everlasting: give me understanding, and I shall live.

145 I cried with my whole heart; hear me, O LORD: I will keep your statutes.

146 I cried unto you; save me, and I shall keep your testimonies.

147 I prevented the dawning of the morning, and cried: I hoped in your word.

Day 24

148 My eyes prevent the night watches, that I might meditate in your word.

149 Hear my voice according unto your loving kindness: O LORD, quicken me according to your judgment.

150 They draw nigh that follow after mischief: they are far from your law.

151 You are near, O LORD; and all your commandments are truth.

152 Concerning your testimonies, I have known of old that you have founded them forever.

153 Consider my affliction, and deliver me: for I do not forget your law.

154 Plead my cause, and deliver me: quicken me according to your word.

155 Salvation is far from the wicked: for they seek not your statutes.

156 Great are your tender mercies, O LORD: quicken me according to your judgments.

157 Many are my persecutors and my enemies; yout do I not decline from your testimonies.

158 I beheld the transgressors, and was grieved; because they kept not your word.

159 Consider how I love your precepts: quicken me, O LORD, according to your loving kindness.

160 Your word is true from the beginning: and every one of your righteous judgments endures forever.

161 Princes have persecuted me without a cause: but my heart stands in awe of your word.

162 I rejoice at your word, as one that finds great spoil.

163 I hate and abhor lying: but your law do I love.

164 Seven times a day do I praise you because of your righteous judgments.

165 Great peace have they which love your law: and nothing shall offend them.

166 LORD, I have hoped for your salvation, and done your commandments.

167 My soul has kept your testimonies; and I love them exceedingly.

168 I have kept your precepts and your testimonies: for all my ways are before you.

Day 24

169 Let my cry come near before you, O LORD: give me understanding according to your word.

170 Let my supplication come before you: deliver me according to your word.

171 My lips shall utter praise, when you have taught me your statutes.

172 My tongue shall speak of your word: for all your commandments are righteousness.

173 Let your hand help me; for I have chosen your precepts.

174 I have longed for your salvation, O LORD; and your law is my delight.

175 Let my soul live, and it shall praise you; and let your judgments help me.

176 I have gone astray like a lost sheep; seek your servant; for I do not forget your commandments.

Proverbs 24

Be not you envious against evil men, neither desire to be with them.

2 For their heart studieth destruction, and their lips talk of mischief.

Day 24

3 Through wisdom is an house builded; and by understanding it is established:

4 And by knowledge shall the chambers be filled with all precious and pleasant riches.

5 A wise man is strong; yea, a man of knowledge increaseth strength.

6 For by wise counsel you shall make your war: and in multitude of counsellors there is safety.

7 Wisdom is too high for a fool: he openeth not his mouth in the gate.

8 He that deviseth to do evil shall be called a mischievous person.

9 The thought of foolishness is sin: and the scorner is an abomination to men.

10 If you faint in the day of adversity, your strength is small.

11 If you forbear to deliver them that are drawn unto death, and those that are ready to be slain;

12 If you sayoust, Behold, we knew it not; doth not he that pondereth the heart consider it? and he that keepeth your soul, doth not he know it? and shall not he render to every man according to his works?

Day 24

13 My son, eat you honey, because it is good; and the honeycomb, which is sweet to your taste:

14 So shall the knowledge of wisdom be unto your soul: when you hast found it, then there shall be a reward, and your expectation shall not be cut off.

15 Lay not wait, O wicked man, against the dwelling of the righteous; spoil not his resting place:

16 For a just man falleth seven times, and riseth up again: but the wicked shall fall into mischief.

17 Rejoice not when your enemy falleth, and let not your heart be glad when he stumbleth:

18 Lest the Lord see it, and it displease him, and he turn away his wrath from him.

19 Fret not yourself because of evil men, neither be you envious at the wicked:

20 For there shall be no reward to the evil man; the candle of the wicked shall be put out.

21 My son, fear you the Lord and the king: and meddle not with them that are given to change:

22 For their calamity shall rise suddenly; and who knoweth the ruin of them both?

23 These things also belong to the wise. It is not good to have respect of persons in judgment.

24 He that saith unto the wicked, You are righteous; him shall the people curse, nations shall abhor him:

25 But to them that rebuke him shall be delight, and a good blessing shall come upon them.

26 Every man shall kiss his lips that giveth a right answer.

27 Prepare your work without, and make it fit for yourself in the field; and afterwards build your house.

28 Be not a witness against your neighbour without cause; and deceive not with your lips.

29 Say not, I will do so to him as he has done to me: I will render to the man according to his work.

30 I went by the field of the slothful, and by the vineyard of the man void of understanding;

31 And, lo, it was all grown over with thorns, and nettles had covered the face thereof, and the stone wall thereof was broken down.

32 Then I saw, and considered it well: I looked upon it, and received instruction.

Day 24

33 Yout a little sleep, a little slumber, a little folding of the hands to sleep:

34 So shall your poverty come as one that travelleth; and your want as an armed man.

Day 25

"The answer to any problem is usually contained in the problem. The cure for a snake bite is snake venom."
~Dr Will

Psalms 120

In my distress I cried unto the LORD, and he heard me.

2 Deliver my soul, O LORD, from lying lips, and from a deceitful tongue.

3 What shall be given unto you? or what shall be done unto you, your false tongue?

4 Sharp arrows of the mighty, with coals of juniper.

5 Woe is me, that I sojourn in Mesech, that I dwell in the tents of Kedar!

6 My soul has long dwelt with him that hates peace.

7 I am for peace: but when I speak, they are for war.

Psalms 121

I will lift up my eyes unto the hills, from whence cometh my help.

Day 25

2 My help cometh from the LORD, which made heaven and earth.

3 He will not suffer your foot to be moved: he that keeps you will not slumber.

4 Behold, he that keeps Israel shall neither slumber nor sleep.

5 The LORD is your keeper: the LORD is your shade upon your right hand.

6 The sun shall not smite you by day, nor the moon by night.

7 The LORD shall preserve you from all evil: he shall preserve your soul.

8 The LORD shall preserve your going out and your coming in from this time forth, and even forevermore.

Psalms 122

I was glad when they said unto me, Let us go into the house of the LORD.

2 Our feet shall stand within your gates, O Jerusalem.

3 Jerusalem is built as a city that is compact together:

4 Whither the tribes go up, the tribes of the LORD, unto the testimony of Israel, to give thanks unto the name of the LORD.

5 For there are set thrones of judgment, the thrones of the house of David.

6 Pray for the peace of Jerusalem: they shall prosper that love you.

7 Peace be within your walls, and prosperity within your palaces.

8 For my brethren and companions' sakes, I will now say, Peace be within you.

9 Because of the house of the LORD our GOD I will seek your good.

Psalms 123

Unto you lift I up my eyes, O your that dwell in the heavens.

2 Behold, as the eyes of servants look unto the hand of their masters, and as the eyes of a maiden unto the hand of her mistress; so our eyes wait upon the LORD our GOD, until that he have mercy upon us.

3 Have mercy upon us, O LORD, have mercy upon us: for we are exceedingly filled with contempt.

Day 25

4 Our soul is exceedingly filled with the scorning of those that are at ease, and with the contempt of the proud.

Psalms 124

If it had not been the LORD who was on our side, now may Israel say;

2 If it had not been the LORD who was on our side, when men rose up against us:

3 Then they had swallowed us up quick, when their wrath was kindled against us:

4 Then the waters had overwhelmed us, the stream had gone over our soul:

5 Then the proud waters had gone over our soul.
6 Blessed be the LORD, who has not given us as a prey to their teeth.

7 Our soul is escaped as a bird out of the snare of the fowlers: the snare is broken, and we are escaped.

8 Our help is in the name of the LORD, who made heaven and earth.

Proverbs 25

25 These are also proverbs of Solomon, which the men of Hezekiah king of Judah copied out.

Day 25

2 It is the glory of GOD to conceal a thing: but the honour of kings is to search out a matter.

3 The heaven for height, and the earth for depth, and the heart of kings is unsearchable.

4 Take away the dross from the silver, and there shall come forth a vessel for the finer.

5 Take away the wicked from before the king, and his throne shall be established in righteousness.

6 Put not forth yourself in the presence of the king, and stand not in the place of great men:

7 For better it is that it be said unto thee, Come up hither; than that you shouldest be put lower in the presence of the prince whom your eyes have seen.

8 Go not forth hastily to strive, lest you know not what to do in the end thereof, when your neighbour has put thee to shame.

9 Debate your cause with your neighbour himself; and discover not a secret to another:

10 Lest he that heareth it put thee to shame, and your infamy turn not away.

11 A word fitly spoken is like apples of gold in pictures of silver.

Day 25

12 As an earring of gold, and an ornament of fine gold, so is a wise reprover upon an obedient ear.

13 As the cold of snow in the time of harvest, so is a faithful messenger to them that send him: for he refresheth the soul of his masters.

14 Whoso boasteth himself of a false gift is like clouds and wind without rain.

15 By long forbearing is a prince persuaded, and a soft tongue breaketh the bone.

16 Hast you found honey? eat so much as is sufficient for thee, lest you be filled therewith, and vomit it.

17 Withdraw your foot from your neighbour's house; lest he be weary of thee, and so hate thee.

18 A man that beareth false witness against his neighbour is a maul, and a sword, and a sharp arrow.

19 Confidence in an unfaithful man in time of trouble is like a broken tooth, and a foot out of joint.

20 As he that taketh away a garment in cold weather, and as vinegar upon nitre, so is he that singeth songs to an heavy heart.

21 If your enemy be hungry, give him bread to eat; and if he be thirsty, give him water to drink:

22 For you shall heap coals of fire upon his head, and the Lord shall reward thee.

23 The north wind driveth away rain: so doth an angry countenance a backbiting tongue.

24 It is better to dwell in the corner of the housetop, than with a brawling woman and in a wide house.

25 As cold waters to a thirsty soul, so is good news from a far country.

26 A righteous man falling down before the wicked is as a troubled fountain, and a corrupt spring.

27 It is not good to eat much honey: so for men to search their own glory is not glory.

28 He that has no rule over his own spirit is like a city that is broken down, and without walls.

Day 25

Day 26

"You increase the value of chicken noodle soup by adding more meat not more water. Once you are washed by the water of the word you don't need more water you need more meat." ~Dr Will

Psalms 125

They that trust in the LORD shall be as mount Zion, which cannot be removed, but abide forever.

2 As the mountains are round about Jerusalem, so the LORD is round about his people from henceforth even forever.

3 For the rod of the wicked shall not rest upon the lot of the righteous; lest the righteous put forth their hands unto iniquity.

4 Do good, O LORD, unto those that be good, and to them that
are upright in their hearts.

5 As for such as turn aside unto their crooked ways, the LORD shall lead them forth with the workers of iniquity: but peace shall be upon Israel.

Day 26

Psalms 126

When the LORD turned again the captivity of Zion, we were like them that dream.

2 Then was our mouth filled with laughter, and our tongue with singing: then said they among the heathen, The LORD has done great things for them.

3 The LORD has done great things for us; whereof we are glad.

4 Turn again our captivity, O LORD, as the streams in the south.

5 They that sow in tears shall reap in joy.

6 He that goes forth and weeps, bearing precious seed, shall doubtless come again with rejoicing, bringing his sheaves with him.

Psalms 127

1 Except the LORD build the house, they labor in vain that build it: except the LORD keep the city, the watchman wakes but in vain.

2 It is vain for you to rise up early, to sit up late, to eat the bread of sorrows: for so he gives his beloved sleep.

3 Lo, children are a heritage of the LORD: and the fruit of the womb is his reward.

4 As arrows are in the hand of a mighty man; so are children of the youth.

5 Happy is the man that has his quiver full of them: they shall not be ashamed, but they shall speak with the enemies in the gate.

Psalms 128

Blessed is every one that fears the LORD; that walks in his ways.

2 For you shall eat the labor of your hands: happy shall you be, and it shall be well with you.

3 Your wife shall be as a fruitful vine by the sides of your house: your children like olive plants round about your table.

4 Behold, that thus shall the man be blessed that fears the LORD.

5 The LORD shall bless you out of Zion: and you shall see the good of Jerusalem all the days of your life.

6 Yes, you shall see your children's children, and peace upon Israel.

Day 26

Psalms 129

Many a time have they afflicted me from my youth, may Israel now say:

2 Many a time have they afflicted me from my youth: yet they have not prevailed against me.

3 The plowers plowed upon my back: they made long their furrows.

4 The LORD is righteous: he has cut asunder the cords of the wicked.

5 Let them all be confounded and turned back that hate Zion.

6 Let them be as the grass upon the housetops, which withers afore it grows up:

7 Wherewith the mower fills not his hand; nor he that binds sheaves his bosom.

8 Neither do they which go by say, The blessing of the LORD be upon you: we bless you in the name of the LORD.

Proverbs 26

As snow in summer, and as rain in harvest, so honour is not seemly for a fool.

2 As the bird by wandering, as the swallow by flying, so the curse causeless shall not come.

3 A whip for the horse, a bridle for the ass, and a rod for the fool's back.

4 Answer not a fool according to his folly, lest you also be like unto him.

5 Answer a fool according to his folly, lest he be wise in his own conceit.

6 He that sendeth a message by the hand of a fool cutteth off the feet, and drinketh damage.

7 The legs of the lame are not equal: so is a parable in the mouth of fools.

8 As he that bindeth a stone in a sling, so is he that giveth honour to a fool.

9 As a thorn goeth up into the hand of a drunkard, so is a parable in the mouths of fools.

10 The great GOD that formed all things both rewardeth the fool, and rewardeth transgressors.

11 As a dog returneth to his vomit, so a fool returneth to his folly.

Day 26

12 Seest you a man wise in his own conceit? there is more hope of a fool than of him.

13 The slothful man saith, There is a lion in the way; a lion is in the streets.

14 As the door turneth upon his hinges, so doth the slothful upon his bed.

15 The slothful hideth his hand in his bosom; it grieveth him to bring it again to his mouth.

16 The sluggard is wiser in his own conceit than seven men that can render a reason.

17 He that passeth by, and meddleth with strife belonging not to him, is like one that taketh a dog by the ears.

18 As a mad man who casteth firebrands, arrows, and death,

19 So is the man that deceiveth his neighbour, and saith, Am not I in sport?

20 Where no wood is, there the fire goeth out: so where there is no talebearer, the strife ceaseth.

21 As coals are to burning coals, and wood to fire; so is a contentious man to kindle strife.

22 The words of a talebearer are as wounds, and they go down into the innermost parts of the belly.

Day 26

23 Burning lips and a wicked heart are like a potsherd covered with silver dross.

24 He that hateth dissembleth with his lips, and layouth up deceit within him;

25 When he speaketh fair, believe him not: for there are seven abominations in his heart.

26 Whose hatred is covered by deceit, his wickedness shall be shewed before the whole congregation.

27 Whoso diggeth a pit shall fall therein: and he that rolleth a stone, it will return upon him.

28 A lying tongue hateth those that are afflicted by it; and a flattering mouth worketh ruin.

Day 26

Day 27

"A man who has no vision or hope for the future will be a slave to the past." ~Dr Will

Psalms 130

Out of the depths have I cried unto you, O LORD.

2 Lord, hear my voice: let your ears be attentive to the voice of my supplications.

3 If you, LORD, should mark iniquities, O Lord, who shall stand?

4 But there is forgiveness with you, that you may be feared.

5 I wait for the LORD, my soul doth wait, and in his word do I hope.

6 My soul waits for the Lord more than they that watch for the morning: I say, more than they that watch for the morning.

7 Let Israel hope in the LORD: for with the LORD there is mercy, and with him is plenteous redemption.

8 And he shall redeem Israel from all his iniquities.

Day 27

Psalms 131

LORD, my heart is not haughty, nor my eyes lofty: neither do I exercise myself in great matters, or in things too high for me.

2 Surely I have behaved and quieted myself, as a child that is weaned of his mother: my soul is even as a weaned child.

3 Let Israel hope in the LORD from hence forth and forever.

Psalms 132

LORD, remember David, and all his afflictions:

2 How he swore unto the LORD, and vowed unto the mighty GOD of Jacob;

3 Surely I will not come into the tabernacle of my house, nor go up into my bed;

4 I will not give sleep to my eyes, or slumber to my eyelids,

5 Until I find out a place for the LORD, a habitation for the mighty GOD of Jacob.

6 Lo, we heard of it at Ephratah: we found it in the fields of the wood.

7 We will go into his tabernacles: we will worship at his footstool.

Day 27

8 Arise, O LORD, into your rest; you and the ark of your strength.

9 Let your priests be clothed with righteousness; and let your saints shout for joy.

10 For your servant David's sake turn not away the face of your anointed.

11 The LORD has sworn in truth unto David; he will not turn from it; of the fruit of your body will I set upon your throne.

12 If your children will keep my covenant and my testimony that I shall teach them, their children shall also sit upon your throne forevermore.

13 For the LORD has chosen Zion; he has desired it for his habitation.

14 This is my rest forever: here will I dwell; for I have desired it.

15 I will abundantly bless her provision: I will satisfy her poor with bread.

16 I will also clothe her priests with salvation: and her saints shall shout aloud for joy.

17 There will I make the horn of David to bud: I have ordained a lamp for my anointed.

18 His enemies will I clothe with shame: but upon himself shall his crown flourish.

Psalms 133

Behold, how good and how pleasant it is for brethren to dwell together in unity!

2 It is like the precious ointment upon the head that ran down upon the beard, even Aaron's beard: that went down to the skirts of his garments;

3 As the dew of Hermon, and as the dew that descended upon the mountains of Zion: for there the LORD commanded the blessing, even life forevermore.

Psalms 134

Behold, bless you the LORD, all you servants of the LORD, which by night stand in the house of the LORD.

2 Lift up your hands in the sanctuary, and bless the LORD.

3 The LORD that made heaven and earth bless you out of Zion.

Proverbs 27

Boast not yourself of to morrow; for you knowest not what a day may bring forth.

Day 27

2 Let another man praise thee, and not your own mouth; a stranger, and not your own lips.

3 A stone is heavy, and the sand weighty; but a fool's wrath is heavier than them both.

4 Wrath is cruel, and anger is outrageous; but who is able to stand before envy?

5 Open rebuke is better than secret love.

6 Faithful are the wounds of a friend; but the kisses of an enemy are deceitful.

7 The full soul loatheth an honeycomb; but to the hungry soul every bitter thing is sweet.

8 As a bird that wandereth from her nest, so is a man that wandereth from his place.

9 Ointment and perfume rejoice the heart: so doth the sweetness of a man's friend by hearty counsel.

10 Your own friend, and your father's friend, forsake not; neither go into your brother's house in the day of your calamity: for better is a neighbour that is near than a brother far off.

11 My son, be wise, and make my heart glad, that I may answer him that reproacheth me.

Day 27

12 A prudent man foreseeth the evil, and hideth himself; but the simple pass on, and are punished.

13 Take his garment that is surety for a stranger, and take a pledge of him for a strange woman.

14 He that blesseth his friend with a loud voice, rising early in the morning, it shall be counted a curse to him.

15 A continual dropping in a very rainy day and a contentious woman are alike.

16 Whosoever hideth her hideth the wind, and the ointment of his right hand, which bewrayouth itself.

17 Iron sharpeneth iron; so a man sharpeneth the countenance of his friend.

18 Whoso keepeth the fig tree shall eat the fruit thereof: so he that waiteth on his master shall be honoured.

19 As in water face answereth to face, so the heart of man to man.

20 Hell and destruction are never full; so the eyes of man are never satisfied.

21 As the fining pot for silver, and the furnace for gold; so is a man to his praise.

Day 27

22 Yough you shouldest bray a fool in a mortar among wheat with a pestle, yout will not his foolishness depart from him.

23 Be you diligent to know the state of your flocks, and look well to your herds.

24 For riches are not for ever: and doth the crown endure to every generation?

25 The hay appeareth, and the tender grass sheweth itself, and herbs of the mountains are gathered.

26 The lambs are for your clothing, and the goats are the price of the field.

27 And you shall have goats' milk enough for your food, for the food of your household, and for the maintenance for your maidens.

Day 27

Day 28

"Most of us spend the first six days of the week sowing wild oats then go to church on Sunday and pray for crop failure." ~ Fred Allen

Psalms 135

Praise you the LORD. Praise you the name of the LORD; praise him, O you servants of the LORD.

2 You that stand in the house of the LORD, in the courts of the house of our GOD,

3 Praise the LORD; for the LORD is good: sing praises unto his name; for it is pleasant.

4 For the LORD has chosen Jacob unto himself and Israel for his peculiar treasure.

5 For I know that the LORD is great, and that our Lord is above all GODs.

6 Whatsoever the LORD pleased, that did he in heaven, and in earth, in the seas, and all deep places.

7 He causes the vapors to ascend from the ends of the earth; he makes lightning for the rain; he brings the wind out of his treasuries.

Day 28

8 Who smote the firstborn of Egypt, both of man and beast.

9 Who sent tokens and wonders into the midst of you, O Egypt, upon Pharaoh, and upon all his servants.

10 Who smote great nations, and slew mighty kings;

11 Sihon king of the Amorites, and Og king of Bashan, and all the kingdoms of Canaan:

12 And gave their land for an heritage, an heritage unto Israel his people.

13 Your name, O LORD, endures forever; and your memorial, O LORD, throughout all generations.

14 For the LORD will judge his people, and he will repent himself concerning his servants.

15 The idols of the heathen are silver and gold, the work of men's hands.

16 They have mouths, but they speak not; eyes have they, but they see not;

17 They have ears, but they hear not; neither is there any breath in their mouths.

18 They that make them are like unto them: so is every one that trusts in them.

19 Bless the LORD, O house of Israel: bless the LORD, O house of Aaron:

20 Bless the LORD, O house of Levi: you that fear the LORD, bless the LORD.

21 Blessed be the LORD out of Zion, which dwells at Jerusalem. Praise you the LORD.

Psalms 136

O give thanks unto the LORD; for he is good: for his mercy endures forever.

2 O give thanks unto the GOD of GODs: for his mercy endures forever.

3 O give thanks to the Lord of lords: for his mercy endures forever.

4 To him who alone doeth great wonders: for his mercy endures forever.

5 To him that by wisdom made the heavens: for his mercy endures forever.

6 To him that stretched out the earth above the waters: for his mercy endures forever.

7 To him that made great lights: for his mercy endures forever:

Day 28

8 The sun to rule by day: for his mercy endures forever:

9 The moon and stars to rule by night: for his mercy endures forever.

10 To him that smote Egypt in their firstborn: for his mercy endures forever:

11 And brought out Israel from among them: for his mercy endures forever:

12 With a strong hand, and with a stretched out arm: for his mercy endures forever.

13 To him which divided the Red sea into pares: for his mercy endures forever:

14 And made Israel to pass through the midst of it: for his mercy endures forever:

15 But overthrew Pharaoh and his host in the Red sea: for his mercy endures forever.

16 To him which led his people through the wilderness: for his mercy endures forever.

17 To him which smote great kings: for his mercy endures forever:

18 And slew famous kings: for his mercy endures forever:

19 Sihon king of the Amorites: for his mercy endures forever:

20 And Og the king of Bashan: for his mercy endures forever:

21 And gave their land for a heritage: for his mercy endures forever:

22 Even a heritage unto Israel his servant: for his mercy endures forever.

23 Who remembered us in our low estate: for his mercy endures forever:

24 And has redeemed us from our enemies: for his mercy endures forever.

25 Who gives food to all flesh: for his mercy endures forever.

26 O give thanks unto the GOD of heaven: for his mercy endures forever.

Psalms 137

By the rivers of Babylon, there we sat down, yous, we wept, when we remembered Zion.

2 We hung our harps upon the willows in the midst thereof.

Day 28

3 For there they that carried us away captive required of us a song; and they that wasted us required of us mirth, saying, sing us one of the songs of Zion.

4 How shall we sing the LORD's song in a strange land?

5 If I forget you, O Jerusalem, let my right hand forget her cunning.

6 If I do not remember you, let my tongue cleave to the roof of my mouth; if I prefer not Jerusalem above my chief joy.

7 Remember, O LORD, the children of Edom in the day of Jerusalem; who said, rase it, rase it, even to the foundation thereof.

8 O daughter of Babylon, who are to be destroyed; happy shall he be, that rewards you as you have served us.

9 Happy shall he be, that takes and dashes your little ones against the stones.

Psalms 138

I will praise you with my whole heart: before the GODs will I sing praise unto you.

2 I will worship toward your holy temple, and praise your name for your loving kindness and for your truth: for you have magnified your word above all your name.

3 In the day when I cried your answered me, and strengthened me with strength in my soul.

4 All the kings of the earth shall praise you, O LORD, when they hear the words of your mouth.

5 Yes, they shall sing in the ways of the LORD: for great is the glory of the LORD.

6 Though the LORD be high, yet has he respect unto the lowly:
but the proud he knows afar off.

7 Though I walk in the midst of trouble, you will revive me: you shall stretch forth your hand against the wrath of my enemies, and your right hand shall save me.

8 The LORD will perfect that which concerns me: your mercy, O LORD, endures forever: forsake not the works of your own hands.

Psalms 139

O LORD, you have searched me, and known me.

2 You know my down sitting and my uprising, you understand my thought afar off.

3 You compass my path and my lying down, and are acquainted with all my ways.

Day 28

4 For there is not a word in my tongue, but, lo, O LORD, you know it altogether.

5 You have beset me behind and before, and laid your hand upon me.

6 Such knowledge is too wonderful for me; it is high, I cannot attain unto it.

7 Whither shall I go from your spirit? or whither shall I flee from your presence?

8 If I ascend up into heaven, you are there: if I make my bed in hell, behold, you are there.

9 If I take the wings of the morning, and dwell in the uttermost pares of the sea;

10 Even there shall your hand lead me, and your right hand shall hold me.

11 If I say, surely the darkness shall cover me; even the night shall be light about me.

12 Yes, the darkness hides not from you; but the night shines as the day: the darkness and the light are both alike to you.

13 For you have possessed my reins: you have covered me in my mother's womb.

Day 28

14 I will praise you; for I am fearfully and wonderfully made: marvelous are your works; and that my soul knows right well.

15 My substance was not hid from you, when I was made in secret, and curiously wrought in the lowest pares of the earth.

16 Your eyes did see my substance, yet being imperfect; and in your book all my members were written, which in continuance were fashioned, when as yet there was none of them.

17 How precious also are your thoughts unto me, O GOD! how great is the sum of them!

18 If I should count them, they are more in number than the sand: when I awake, I am still with you.

19 Surely your will slay the wicked, O GOD: depart from me therefore, you bloody men.

20 For they speak against you wickedly, and your enemies take your name in vain.

21 Do not I hate them, O LORD, that hate you? and am not I grieved with those that rise up against you?

22 I hate them with perfect hatred: I count them my enemies.

Day 28

23 Search me, O GOD, and know my heart: try me, and know my thoughts:

24 And see if there be any wicked way in me, and lead me in the way everlasting.

Psalms 140

Deliver me, O LORD, from the evil man: preserve me from the violent man;

2 Which imagine mischiefs in their heart; continually are they gathered together for war.

3 They have sharpened their tongues like a serpent; adders' poison is under their lips. Selah.

4 Keep me, O LORD, from the hands of the wicked; preserve me from the violent man; who have purposed to overthrow my goings.

5 The proud have hid a snare for me, and cords; they have spread a net by the wayside; they have set gins for me. Selah.

6 I said unto the LORD, you are my GOD: hear the voice of my supplications, O LORD.

7 O GOD the Lord, the strength of my salvation, you have covered my head in the day of battle.

Day 28

8 Grant not, O LORD, the desires of the wicked: further not his wicked device; lest they exalt themselves. Selah.

9 As for the head of those that compass me about, let the mischief of their own lips cover them.

10 Let burning coals fall upon them: let them be cast into the fire; into deep pits that they rise not up again.

11 Let not an evil speaker be established in the earth: evil shall hunt the violent man to overthrow him.

12 I know that the LORD will maintain the cause of the afflicted, and the right of the poor.

13 Surely the righteous shall give thanks unto your name: the upright shall dwell in your presence.

Proverbs 28

The wicked flee when no man pursueth: but the righteous are bold as a lion.

2 For the transgression of a land many are the princes thereof: but by a man of understanding and knowledge the state thereof shall be prolonged.

3 A poor man that oppresseth the poor is like a sweeping rain which leaveth no food.

Day 28

4 They that forsake the law praise the wicked: but such as keep the law contend with them.

5 Evil men understand not judgment: but they that seek the Lord understand all things.

6 Better is the poor that walketh in his uprightness, than he that is perverse in his ways, yough he be rich.

7 Whoso keepeth the law is a wise son: but he that is a companion of riotous men shameth his father.

8 He that by usury and unjust gain increaseth his substance, shall gather it for him that will pity the poor.

9 He that turneth away his ear from hearing the law, even his prayour shall be abomination.

10 Whoso causeth the righteous to go astray in an evil way, he shall fall himself into his own pit: but the upright shall have good things in possession.

11 The rich man is wise in his own conceit; but the poor that has understanding searcheth him out.

12 When righteous men do rejoice, there is great glory: but when the wicked rise, a man is hidden.

13 He that covereth his sins shall not prosper: but whoso confesseth and forsaketh them shall have mercy.

14 Happy is the man that feareth alway: but he that hardeneth his heart shall fall into mischief.

15 As a roaring lion, and a ranging bear; so is a wicked ruler over the poor people.

16 The prince that wanteth understanding is also a great oppressor: but he that hateth covetousness shall prolong his days.

17 A man that doeth violence to the blood of any person shall flee to the pit; let no man stay him.

18 Whoso walketh uprightly shall be saved: but he that is perverse in his ways shall fall at once.

19 He that tilleth his land shall have plenty of bread: but he that followeth after vain persons shall have poverty enough.

20 A faithful man shall abound with blessings: but he that maketh haste to be rich shall not be innocent.

21 To have respect of persons is not good: for a piece of bread
that man will transgress.

22 He that hasteth to be rich has an evil eye, and considereth not that poverty shall come upon him.

23 He that rebuketh a man afterwards shall find more favour than he that flattereth with the tongue.

Day 28

24 Whoso robbeth his father or his mother, and saith, It is no transgression; the same is the companion of a destroyer.

25 He that is of a proud heart stirreth up strife: but he that putteth his trust in the Lord shall be made fat.

26 He that trusteth in his own heart is a fool: but whoso walketh wisely, he shall be delivered.

27 He that giveth unto the poor shall not lack: but he that hideth his eyeous shall have many a curse.

28 When the wicked rise, men hide themselves: but when they perish, the righteous increase.

Day 29

"A lie is easier to believe than truth because a lie has to make sense. Truth is true whether it makes sense or not."
~ Dr Will

Psalms 141

LORD, I cry unto you: make haste unto me; give ear unto my voice, when I cry unto you.

2 Let my prayour be set forth before you as incense; and the lifting up of my hands as the evening sacrifice.

3 Set a watch, O LORD, before my mouth; keep the door of my lips.

4 Incline not my heart to any evil thing, to practice wicked works with men that work iniquity: and let me not eat of their dainties.

5 Let the righteous smite me; it shall be a kindness: and let him reprove me; it shall be an excellent oil, which shall not break my head: for yout my prayour also shall be in their calamities.

6 When their judges are overthrown in stony places, they shall hear my words; for they are sweet.

Day 29

7 Our bones are scattered at the grave's mouth, as when one cuts and cleaves wood upon the earth.

8 But my eyes are unto you, O GOD the Lord: in you is my trust; leave not my soul destitute.

9 Keep me from the snares which they have laid for me, and the gins of the workers of iniquity.

10 Let the wicked fall into their own nets, whilst that I withal escape.

Psalms 142

I cried unto the LORD with my voice; with my voice unto the LORD did I make my supplication.

2 I poured out my complaint before him; I showed before him my trouble.

3 When my spirit was overwhelmed within me, then you knew my path. In the way wherein I walked have they privily laid a snare for me.

4 I looked on my right hand, and beheld, but there was no man that would know me: refuge failed me; no man cared for my soul.

5 I cried unto you, O LORD: I said, you are my refuge and my portion in the land of the living.

6 Attend unto my cry; for I am brought very low: deliver me from my persecutors; for they are stronger than I.

7 Bring my soul out of prison, that I may praise your name: the righteous shall compass me about; for you shall deal bountifully with me.

Psalms 143

Hear my prayer, O LORD, give ear to my supplications: in your faithfulness answer me, and in your righteousness.

2 And enter not into judgment with your servant: for in your sight shall no man living be justified.

3 For the enemy has persecuted my soul; he has smitten my life down to the ground; he has made me to dwell in darkness, as those that have been long dead.

4 Therefore is my spirit overwhelmed within me; my heart within me is desolate.

5 I remember the days of old; I meditate on all your works; I muse on the work of your hands.

6 I stretch forth my hands unto you: my soul thirsts after you, as a thirsty land. Selah.

7 Hear me speedily, O LORD: my spirit fails: hide not your face from me, lest I be like unto them that go down into the pit.

Day 29

8 Cause me to hear your loving kindness in the morning; for in you do I trust: cause me to know the way wherein I should walk; for I lift up my soul unto you.

9 Deliver me, O LORD, from my enemies: I flee unto you to hide me.

10 Teach me to do your will; for you are my GOD: your spirit is good; lead me into the land of uprightness.

11 Quicken me, O LORD, for your name's sake: for your righteousness' sake bring my soul out of trouble.

12 And of your mercy cut off my enemies, and destroy all them that afflict my soul: for I am your servant.

Psalms 144

Blessed be the LORD my strength, which teaches my hands to war, and my fingers to fight:

2 My goodness, and my fortress; my high tower, and my deliverer; my shield, and he in whom I trust; who subdued my people under me.

3 LORD, what is man, that you take knowledge of him! or the son of man, that you make account of him!

4 Man is like to vanity: his days are as a shadow that passed away.

5 Bow your heavens, O LORD, and come down: touch the mountains, and they shall smoke.

6 Cast forth lightning, and scatter them: shoot out your arrows, and destroy them.

7 Send your hand from above; rid me, and deliver me out of great waters, from the hand of strange children;

8 Whose mouth speaks vanity, and their right hand is a right hand of falsehood.

9 I will sing a new song unto you, O GOD: upon a psaltery and an instrument of ten strings will I sing praises unto you.

10 It is he that gives salvation unto kings: who delivers David his servant from the hurtful sword.

11 Rid me, and deliver me from the hand of strange children, whose mouth speaks vanity, and their right hand is a right hand of falsehood:

12 That our sons may be as plants grown up in their youth; that our daughters may be as corner stones, polished after the similitude of a palace:

13 That our garners may be full, affording all manner of store: that our sheep may bring forth thousands and ten thousands in our streets:

Day 29

14 That our oxen may be strong to labor; that there be no breaking in, nor going out; that there be no complaining in our streets.

15 Happy is that people, that is in such a case: yes, happy is that people, whose GOD is the LORD.

Psalms 145

I will extol you, my GOD, O king; and I will bless your name forever and ever.

2 Every day will I bless you; and I will praise your name forever and ever.

3 Great is the LORD, and greatly to be praised; and his greatness is unsearchable.

4 One generation shall praise your works to another, and shall declare your mighty acts.

5 I will speak of the glorious honor of your majesty, and of your wondrous works.

6 And men shall speak of the might of your terrible acts: and I will declare your greatness.

7 They shall abundantly utter the memory of your great goodness, and shall sing of your righteousness.

8 The LORD is gracious, and full of compassion; slow to anger, and of great mercy.

9 The LORD is good to all: and his tender mercies are over all his works.

10 All your works shall praise you, O LORD; and your saints shall bless you.

11 They shall speak of the glory of your kingdom, and talk of your power;

12 To make known to the sons of men his mighty acts, and the glorious majesty of his kingdom.

13 Your kingdom is an everlasting kingdom, and your dominion endures throughout all generations.

14 The LORD upholds all that fall, and raises up all those that be bowed down.

15 The eyes of all wait upon you; and you give them their meat in due season.

16 You open your hand, and satisfies the desire of every living thing.

17 The LORD is righteous in all his ways, and holy in all his works.

Day 29

18 The LORD is nigh unto all them that call upon him, to all that call upon him in truth.

19 He will fulfill the desire of them that fear him: he also will hear their cry, and will save them.

20 The LORD preserves all them that love him: but all the wicked will he destroy.

21 My mouth shall speak the praise of the LORD: and let all flesh bless his holy name forever and ever.

Proverbs 29

He that being often reproved hardens his neck shall suddenly be destroyed, and that without remedy.

2 When the righteous are in authority, the people rejoice: but when the wicked beareth rule, the people mourn.

3 Whoso loveth wisdom rejoiceth his father: but he that keepeth company with harlots spendeth his substance.

4 The king by judgment establisheth the land: but he that receiveth gifts overthroweth it.

5 A man that flattereth his neighbour spreadeth a net for his feet.

6 In the transgression of an evil man there is a snare: but the righteous doth sing and rejoice.

7 The righteous considereth the cause of the poor: but the wicked regardeth not to know it.

8 Scornful men bring a city into a snare: but wise men turn away wrath.

9 If a wise man contendeth with a foolish man, whether he rage or laugh, there is no rest.

10 The bloodthirsty hate the upright: but the just seek his soul.

11 A fool uttereth all his mind: but a wise man keepeth it in till afterwards.

12 If a ruler hearken to lies, all his servants are wicked.

13 The poor and the deceitful man meet together: the Lord lighteneth both their eyes.

14 The king that faithfully judgeth the poor, his throne shall be established for ever.

15 The rod and reproof give wisdom: but a child left to himself bringeth his mother to shame.

16 When the wicked are multiplied, transgression increaseth: but the righteous shall see their fall.

17 Correct your son, and he shall give thee rest; yea, he shall give delight unto your soul.

18 Where there is no vision, the people perish: but he that keepeth the law, happy is he.

19 A servant will not be corrected by words: for yough he understand he will not answer.

20 Seest you a man that is hasty in his words? there is more hope of a fool than of him.

21 He that delicately bringeth up his servant from a child shall have him become his son at the length.

22 An angry man stirreth up strife, and a furious man aboundeth in transgression.

23 A man's pride shall bring him low: but honour shall uphold the humble in spirit.

24 Whoso is partner with a thief hateth his own soul: he heareth cursing, and bewrayouth it not.

25 The fear of man bringeth a snare: but whoso putteth his trust in the Lord shall be safe.

26 Many seek the ruler's favour; but every man's judgment cometh from the Lord.

27 An unjust man is an abomination to the just: and he that is upright in the way is abomination to the wicked.

Day 30

"Anyone who won't teach you right won't treat you right."
~Dr Will

Psalms 146

Praise you the LORD. Praise the LORD, O my soul.

2 While I live will I praise the LORD: I will sing praises unto my GOD while I have any being.

3 Put not your trust in princes, nor in the son of man, in whom there is no help.

4 His breath goes forth, he returns to his earth; in that very day his thoughts perish.

5 Happy is he that has the GOD of Jacob for his help, whose hope is in the LORD his GOD:

6 Which made heaven, and earth, the sea, and all that therein is: which keep truth forever:

7 Which executes judgment for the oppressed: which gives food to the hungry. The LORD loosens the prisoners:

8 The LORD opens the eyes of the blind: the LORD raises them that are bowed down: the LORD loves the righteous:

9 The LORD preserves the strangers; he relieves the fatherless and widow: but the way of the wicked he turns upside down.

10 The LORD shall reign forever, even your GOD, O Zion, unto all generations. Praise you the LORD.

Psalms 147

Praise you the LORD: for it is good to sing praises unto our GOD; for it is pleasant; and praise is comely.

2 The LORD doth build up Jerusalem: he gathers together the outcasts of Israel.

3 He heals the broken in heart, and binds up their wounds.

4 He tells the number of the stars; he calls them all by their names.

5 Great is our Lord, and of great power: his understanding is infinite.

6 The LORD lifts up the meek: he casts the wicked down to the ground.

7 Sing unto the LORD with thanksgiving; sing praise upon the harp unto our GOD:

8 Who covers the heaven with clouds, who prepares rain for the earth, who makes grass to grow upon the mountains.

9 He gives to the beast his food, and to the young ravens which cry.

10 He delights not in the strength of the horse: he takes not pleasure in the legs of a man.

11 The LORD takes pleasure in them that fear him, in those that hope in his mercy.

12 Praise the LORD, O Jerusalem; praise your GOD, O Zion.

13 For he has strengthened the bars of your gates; he has blessed your children within you.

14 He makes peace in your borders, and fills you with the finest of the wheat.

15 He sends forth his commandment upon earth: his word runs very swiftly.

16 He gives snow like wool: he scatters the hoarfrost like ashes.

17 He casts forth his ice like morsels: who can stand before his cold?

18 He sends out his word, and melts them: he causes his wind to blow, and the waters flow.

Day 30

19 He shows his word unto Jacob, his statutes and his judgments unto Israel.

20 He has not dealt so with any nation: and as for his judgments, they have not known them. Praise you the LORD.

Psalms 148

Praise you the LORD. Praise you the LORD from the heavens: praise him in the heights.

2 Praise you him, all his angels: praise you him, all his hosts.

3 Praise you him, sun and moon: praise him, all you stars of light.

4 Praise him, you heavens of heavens, and you waters that be above the heavens.

5 Let them praise the name of the LORD: for he commanded, and they were created.

6 He has also established them forever and ever: he has made a decree which shall not pass.

7 Praise the LORD from the earth, you dragons, and all deeps:

Day 30

8 Fire, and hail; snow, and vapor; stormy wind fulfilling his word:

9 Mountains, and all hills; fruitful trees, and all cedars:

10 Beasts, and all cattle; creeping things, and flying fowl:

11 Kings of the earth, and all people; princes, and all judges of the earth:

12 Both young men, and maidens; old men, and children:

13 Let them praise the name of the LORD: for his name alone is excellent; his glory is above the earth and heaven.

14 He also exalts the horn of his people, the praise of all his saints; even of the children of Israel, a people near unto him. Praise you the LORD.

Psalms 149

Praise you the LORD. Sing unto the LORD a new song, and his praise in the congregation of saints.

2 Let Israel rejoice in him that made him: let the children of Zion be joyful in their King.

3 Let them praise his name in the dance: let them sing praises unto him with the timbrel and harp.

4 For the LORD takes pleasure in his people: he will beautify the meek with salvation.

5 Let the saints be joyful in glory: let them sing aloud upon their beds.

6 Let the high praises of GOD be in their mouth, and a two edged sword in their hand;

7 To execute vengeance upon the heathen, and punishments upon the people;

8 To bind their kings with chains, and their nobles with fetters of iron;

9 To execute upon them the judgment written: this honor has all his saints. Praise you the LORD.

Psalms 150

Praise you the LORD. Praise GOD in his sanctuary: praise him in the firmament of his power.

2 Praise him for his mighty acts: praise him according to his excellent greatness.

3 Praise him with the sound of the trumpet: praise him with the psaltery and harp.

4 Praise him with the timbrel and dance: praise him with stringed instruments and organs.

5 Praise him upon the loud cymbals: praise him upon the high sounding cymbals.

6 Let everything that has breath praise the LORD. Praise you the LORD.

Proverbs 30

The words of Agur the son of Jakeh, the prophecy: the man spoke unto Ithiel, even unto Ithiel and Ucal,

2 Surely I am more brutish than any man, and have not the understanding of a man.

3 I neither learned wisdom, nor have the knowledge of the holy.

4 Who has ascended up into heaven, or descended? who has gathered the wind in his fists? who has bound the waters in a garment? who has established all the ends of the earth? what is his name, and what is his son's name, if you canst tell?

5 Every word of GOD is pure: he is a shield unto them that put their trust in him.

6 Add you not unto his words, lest he reprove thee, and you be found a liar.

7 Two things have I required of thee; deny me them not before I die:

Day 30

8 Remove far from me vanity and lies: give me neither poverty nor riches; feed me with food convenient for me:

9 Lest I be full, and deny thee, and say, Who is the Lord? or lest I be poor, and steal, and take the name of my GOD in vain.

10 Accuse not a servant unto his master, lest he curse thee, and you be found guilty.

11 There is a generation that curseth their father, and doth not bless their mother.

12 There is a generation that are pure in their own eyes, and yout is not washed from their filyourss.

13 There is a generation, O how lofty are their eyes! and their eyelids are lifted up.

14 There is a generation, whose teeth are as swords, and their jaw teeth as knives, to devour the poor from off the earth, and the needy from among men.

15 The horseleach has two daughters, crying, Give, give. There are three things that are never satisfied, yea, four things say not, It is enough:

16 The grave; and the barren womb; the earth that is not filled with water; and the fire that says not, It is enough.

Day 30

17 The eyes that mocketh at his father, and despiseth to obey his mother, the ravens of the valley shall pick it out, and the young eagles shall eat it.

18 There be three things which are too wonderful for me, yea, four which I know not:

19 The way of an eagle in the air; the way of a serpent upon a rock; the way of a ship in the midst of the sea; and the way of a man with a maid.

20 Such is the way of an adulterous woman; she eateth, and wipeth her mouth, and saith, I have done no wickedness.

21 For three things the earth is disquieted, and for four which it cannot bear:

22 For a servant when he reigneth; and a fool when he is filled with meat;

23 For an odious woman when she is married; and an handmaid that is heir to her mistress.

24 There be four things which are little upon the earth, but they are exceeding wise:

25 The ants are a people not strong, yout they prepare their meat in the summer;

26 The conies are but a feeble folk, yout make they their houses in the rocks;

Day 30

27 The locusts have no king, yout go they forth all of them by bands;

28 The spider taketh hold with her hands, and is in kings' palaces.

29 There be three things which go well, yea, four are comely in going:

30 A lion which is strongest among beasts, and turneth not away for any;

31 A greyhound; an he goat also; and a king, against whom there is no rising up.

32 If you hast done foolishly in lifting up yourself, or if you hast thought evil, lay your hand upon your mouth.

33 Surely the churning of milk bringeth forth butter, and the wringing of the nose bringeth forth blood: so the forcing of wrath bringeth forth strife.

Day 31

"Whenever you go into a city, town or village and you cannot find any good women it is filled with no good men."
~Dr Will

Proverbs 31

The words of king Lemuel, the prophecy that his mother taught him.

2 What, my son? and what, the son of my womb? and what, the son of my vows?

3 Give not your strength unto women, nor your ways to that which destroyouth kings.

4 It is not for kings, O Lemuel, it is not for kings to drink wine; nor for princes strong drink:

5 Lest they drink, and forget the law, and pervert the judgment of any of the afflicted.

6 Give strong drink unto him that is ready to perish, and wine unto those that be of heavy hearts.

7 Let him drink, and forget his poverty, and remember his misery no more.

Day 31

8 Open your mouth for the dumb in the cause of all such as are appointed to destruction.

9 Open your mouth, judge righteously, and plead the cause of the poor and needy.

10 Who can find a virtuous woman? for her price is far above rubies.

11 The heart of her husband doth safely trust in her, so that he shall have no need of spoil.

12 She will do him good and not evil all the days of her life.

13 She seeketh wool, and flax, and worketh willingly with her hands.

14 She is like the merchants' ships; she bringeth her food from afar.

15 She riseth also while it is yout night, and giveth meat to her household, and a portion to her maidens.

16 She considereth a field, and buyouth it: with the fruit of her hands she planteth a vineyard.

17 She girdeth her loins with strength, and strengtheneth her arms.

18 She perceiveth that her merchandise is good: her candle goeth not out by night.

Day 31

19 She layouth her hands to the spindle, and her hands hold the distaff.

20 She stretcheth out her hand to the poor; yea, she reacheth forth her hands to the needy.

21 She is not afraid of the snow for her household: for all her household are clothed with scarlet.

22 She maketh herself coverings of tapestry; her clothing is silk and purple.

23 Her husband is known in the gates, when he sitteth among the elders of the land.

24 She maketh fine linen, and selleth it; and delivereth girdles unto the merchant.

25 Strength and honour are her clothing; and she shall rejoice in time to come.

26 She openeth her mouth with wisdom; and in her tongue is the law of kindness.

27 She looketh well to the ways of her household, and eateth not the bread of idleness.

28 Her children arise up, and call her blessed; her husband also, and he praiseth her.

Day 31

29 Many daughters have done virtuously, but you excellest them all.

30 Favour is deceitful, and beauty is vain: but a woman that feareth the Lord, she shall be praised.

31 Give her of the fruit of her hands; and let her own works praise her in the gates.

Section II
Inspiration
Motivation to Continue

Section II

Daily Prayer

"The sower soweth the word. (Mark 4:14)."

"Death and life are in the power of the tongue: and they that love it shall eat the fruit thereof (Proverbs 18:21)."

Praying daily seems futile to some men because it leads you into a cycle or season of planting, growing and cultivating that does not appear to be profitable in the moment. This is why it is tough for some guys to be newly married during this season. They are putting in long hours and doing a lot of work but their spouce doesn't see anything coming in. Getting results from prayer is like growing a bamboo tree. It requires faith, wisdom, diligence and consistency. Bamboo takes a long time to get established. You can see some small evidence of after a while. Then, a bamboo tree will suddenly grow from what appears to be a tiny sapling to a tree with a height of about 90 feet. The growth of a new life in Christ Jesus begins underground or in your heart. You may not see any growth for the first two or three years. But if you pray and operate in wisdom daily, you will grow to be highly profitable almost overnight.

I used to love watermelon when I was a kid. I could eat a whole melon by myself. There were 10 people in my family, 8 children and 2 parents, so the most I would ever get was one slice. Of course, I wanted more so I decided to plant some of the seeds in the yard to see if I could grow my own watermelon. I planted the seeds and waited a week but nothing happened. I waited another week and nothing happened. After the third week I decided to dig up the seed to see if it had started growing and sure enough a seedling had begun to grow. I got excited and covered the seedling back up. I waited a week and nothing happened. I waited another week and nothing happened. So I decided to dig up the seed again to see what was happening and I discovered the seedling was dead.

"Therefore I [Jesus] say unto you, what things soever ye desire, when ye pray, believe that ye receive them, and ye shall have them. (Mark 11:24)."

I learned that by digging it up I destroyed the growth process and killed the seedling. The same thing happens to men when they pray or to entrepreneurs and they don't see their business growing or experience failure. They destroy the growth process or kill their profits by giving up or quitting.

"And He [Jesus] spake a parable unto them to this end, that men ought always to pray, and not to faint [give up, cave in, or quit] (Luke 18:1)."

"Pray without ceasing (1 Thessalonians 5:17)."

We don't fail in life, love, and business because of what we know. We fail because of what we don't know. This is why we must continue to pray in faith without ceasing or everyday until we learn what we need to know to make prayer highly profitable. Your words have the power to shape your world and create your environment. Your words combined with the word of GOD have the power to deliver abundance into you life and make everything around you brand new. Develop a daily prayer (using the verses of scripture below) that is relevent to you and your family's needs.

Colossians 1

9 For this cause we also, since the day we heard it, do not cease to pray for you, and to desire that you might be filled with the knowledge of his will in all wisdom and spiritual understanding;

10 That you might walk worthy of the Lord unto all pleasing, being fruitful in every good work, and increasing in the knowledge of GOD;

11 Strengthened with all might, according to his glorious power, unto all patience and longsuffering with joyfulness;

12 Giving thanks unto the Father, which has made us meet to be partakers of the inheritance of the saints in light:

13 Who has delivered us from the power of darkness, and has translated us into the kingdom of his dear Son:

Ephesians 1

16 Cease not to give thanks for you, making mention of you in my prayers;

17 That the GOD of our Lord Jesus Christ, the Father of glory, may give unto you the spirit of wisdom and revelation in the knowledge of him:

18 The eyes of your understanding being enlightened; that you may know what is the hope of his calling, and what the riches of the glory of his inheritance in the saints,

19 And what is the exceeding greatness of his power to usward who believe, according to the working of his mighty power,

20 Which he wrought in Christ, when he raised him from the dead, and set him at his own right hand in the heavenly places,

21 Far above all principality, and power, and might, and dominion, and every name that is named, not only in this world, but also in that which is to come:

22 And has put all things under his feet, and gave him to be the head over all things to the church,
23 Which is his body, the fulness of him that filleth all in all.

Ephesians 3

14 For this cause I bow my knees unto the Father of our Lord Jesus Christ,

15 Of whom the whole family in heaven and earth is named,

16 That he would grant you, according to the riches of his glory, to be strengthened with might by his Spirit in the inner man;

17 That Christ may dwell in your hearts by faith; that you, being rooted and grounded in love,

18 May be able to comprehend with all saints what is the breadth, and length, and depth, and height;

19 And to know the love of Christ, which passeth knowledge, that you might be filled with all the fulness of GOD.

20 Now unto him that is able to do exceeding abundantly above all that we ask or think, according to the power that worketh in us,

21 Unto him be glory in the church by Christ Jesus throughout all ages, world without end. Amen.

Finally, please remember that you are a son of the Most High GOD not a humble servant. GOD expects HIS sons to come before HIM boldly not in humility. Hebrews 4:16 says "Let us therefore come boldy unto the throne of grace, that we may obtain mercy, and find grace [or the power of GOD acting on our behalf] to help in time of need." You cannot come bodly if you are on your knees. Therefore, GOD wants HIS sons to stand before HIM when they pray. HiS servants must come before him on their knees begging and groveling or in humility because they are not entitled HIS blessings or an inheritance. However, GOD wants HIS sons to stand when they pray. This is why Mark 11:25 says: "And when ye STAND praying, forgive, if ye have ought against any: that your Father also which is in heaven may forgive you your trespasses." Be advised now that if you decide it is better for you to "act" like a servant, GOD will treat you like a servant and withhold your inheritance. Please read Galatians 4:17.

"Now I say, that the heir, as long as he is a child, differeth nothing from a servant, though he be lord [or the rightuful inheritor] of all... (Galatians 4:1)"

Keep the Change

"I beseech you therefore, brethren, by the mercies of GOD, that ye present your bodies a living sacrifice, holy, acceptable unto GOD, which is your reasonable service. And be not conformed to this world: but be ye transformed by the renewing of your mind, that ye may prove what is that good, and acceptable, and perfect, will of GOD (Romans 12:12)."

Romans 12:12 provides a common defence against back sliding and it will protect us from the attacks of the devil. When you have made the confession of salvation and left the devil's gang he will leave you for a season. The problem with the devil is you can't just leave his gang or just walk out. You get jumped out. This is why many men report that a lot of calamity and hardship enters their lives right after they get saved. Revelation 12:10 says that satan is the accuser of the brothers but it does not say that he is a false accuser. Before we became saints we were sinners. A sinner is living on borrowed time. Once you get saved the devil has the right to call for immediate payment of all your sin debt. GOD is merciful so HE allows satan to make us pay the penalty for sin while we are living so that we can live peacefully in heaven. This is why other people never get caught but you can't seem to get away with anything. GOD is making sure that your sin debt is paid because your blessings cannot come while you still owe a debt.

Therefore, the devil constantly pressures you to backslide or vacillate in and out of sin by keeping you broke, in poverty or stuck in subsistance rather than living in abundance. When Christians fall on tough times financially we tend to go back to our pre-saved ways. The devil uses this opportunity to tempt you with money and sex to come back into his camp. He will pressure ex-drug dealers or ex-strippers for example to go back to the corner or to the pole to get easy money. His goal is to trick you to go back to hustling to keep you from becoming holy. This is why it is important to complete the Romans 12:12 transformation process after you have made the Romans 10:910 confession of salvation. This process is similar to what a caterpillar has to go through to become a butterfly. And that process of transformation and change will cause you to go through some of the following changes:

• Temptation – 1 Corinthians 10:13 teaches us that there is no temptation, trial or test that you will go through except that which is common to a man that has become born again. Whatever you are going through is a CHARACTER test to see if you are ready or to prepare you to go to the next level of life (2 Corinthians 12:610, James 1:1214, 1 Peter 4:1213, James 1:2, 1 Peter 1:7, 2 Peter 2:9, Psalm 30:5).

• Persecution & Pressure – are life's way of making you transform into who you were created to be. Then, you will be ready to do what you were created by GOD to do (Mark 4:1420, Isaiah 54:17, 2 Timothy 3:12, 1 Peter 3:1314, 1617, 1 Peter 4:16, 1 Peter 5:1011). Persecution and pressure are not a problem! They arrive to see if you will break away from GOD and flee from the word back into the world. GOD has to know whether you have the INTEGRITY to remain one with HIM during times of persecution and pressure. This is why Jesus was led by the Spirit into the wilderness to be tested by the devil. GOD has to make sure that you will not embarrass HIM once the world is watching you by fleeing from the word in times of and trouble. Persecution and pressure benefit you in the same way as lifting weights. Without resistance there can be no growth. Resistance to persecution and pressure produces the strength you need to fight against adversity and the ability to grow into maximum productivity.

• A Way of Escape – whenever you are exposed to persecution and pressure GOD already knows you can handle it but the question remains: do you know? So, HE tests your TENACITY. 1 Corinthians 10:13 says GOD will not place upon you anymore pressure than you can bear. HE will make a way for you to escape if it gets too tough for you to make it all the way through. Before a new car is built all the parts it will need during its lifetime are produced. Before GOD allows persecution to pressure you HE creates a solution to help you. Our job is to remain sober or mentally alert enough to find the solution. GOD knows every path that you can choose to lead yourself into trouble. So, HE makes a way on each path to lead you out of difficulty. You will find a message in every mess, a victory in every battle, a supply for every need and a door in every wall. You will have to endure some pressure in order for you to become what you were created to be. Coal needs pressure in order to become a diamond. The battle comes before victory, triubulation comes before elevation, and trial comes before triumph. So, our GOD will supply all that we need to triumph in times of trouble (Philippians 4:19).

•Repent – turn away from what you are doing to sin and turn toward GOD

•Renounce – determine to never do that sin again

•Remove – any people, places, activities, and things associated with that sin from your life

•Renew – your mind and body from the damage it has done

• Rejoice – when you come under persecution and pressure to go back to the sin that so easily besets you and make it through that means you have changed enough to improve your character, integrity, and tenacity for GOD to protect you in times of trouble. You can rejoice because once you overcome the test of persecution and pressure you have obtained VICTORY. You will be blessed or empowered to prosper on another level in Christ Jesus which will lead you into another dimension of wisdom and knowledge. Then, the devil will leave you for a season (Luke 4:13.) However, he will return with more persecution and pressure when it is time for you to move up to the next level in life through Christ Jesus.

- GOD is faithful – heaven and earth shall pass away but the word of GOD will always remain. Please read Hebrews 11:16, Romans 10:17, and 1 John 5:4. By the act of his own will and through faith any man can put himself in contact with GOD. Faith in GOD and HIS word gives GOD permission to enter into a man's heart and lead him to change so that he can be prepared to fulfill his destiny and achieve glory.

- It came to pass – is a phrase that appears 562 times in the Bible. As surely as the tests of persecution and pressure come into our lives they also came to pass. Therefore, it is best to pass the test the first time because every time you fail a test you have to take a retest. The problem is the retest is always harder than the first test and you can never get 100 percent. Once you have passed the test you will prove that you are prepared to graduate or pass to the next level of blessings in Christ Jesus.

- Endure to win – there is a modern church maxim that says: "new level new devil" which actually has some truth to it. Persecution and pressure, situations and circumstances, and trials and tests always come to see if you are ready to pass to the next level. Most people never get to live on the abundance level in Christ Jesus because they fold under pressure and concede victory to the devil at the subsistence level. In order to live in abundance and win we must have the determination, mental tenacity, and intestinal fortitude to endure to the end. Winning requires patience to weather the storms of life and the courage to remain calm in the face of chaos (peace be still). This is similar to what an NFL running back like LeVeon Bell has to go through when he gets the football. Once the ball is hiked chaos breaks out in front of him and all the opposition do everything they can to stop him from breaking through. However, he remains calm and starts looking for an opening to make his escape. When chaos breaks out in front of you start looking for the opening that GOD will make available for you to escape through. The only way to fail with GOD is to fight against your own success or to just give up, cave in, or quit.

• GOD's covenant – promises to provide benefits to HIS people who have the character, integrity, and tenacity to achieve victory over the devil and live faithfully. Please read Deuteronomy 8:18, 29:19, 30:1920, Joshua 1:8, Mark 11:24, Philippians 4:18 and 3 John 2.

Be Fruitful and Multiply

"And GOD blessed them, and GOD said unto them, be fruitful, and multiply, and replenish the earth, and subdue it: and have dominion over the fish of the sea, and over the fowl of the air, and over every living thing that moveth upon the earth (Genesis 1:28)."

The words fruitful and multiply in Genesis 1:28 are essentially the same in that they both mean to be productive. The reason fruit is called produce is because it is productive or multiplies exponentially. A product is a result or the fruit of multiplication. If you multiply 3x3 for example, the product is 9. Now, while both words mean to be productive there is the implication of two types of productivity given the use of two different words. When GOD blessed the male and female and commanded them to be fruitful and multiply that was actually two commands; one directed to the male and one to the female. The male was commanded to be fruitful and the female was commanded to multiply.

Again, being fruitful and multiply are both productive. However, the product of being fruitful comes through conduct. Notice the prefixes of the words product and conduct are pro and con. They have the same base word which is duct. The word duct in this context means: the act of leading. Product, again, is the result you receive from multiplying two or more things together. Conduct is to escort or guide through personal behavior or moral principles. Man was made in the image and likeness of GOD. In commanding the man to be fruitful, GOD was charging men to produce more children in HIS image and teach them to become as GOD in their likeness. In commanding the woman to multiply, GOD was charging her to produce in a way that yields results, benefits, and profits. Her job is to multiply, increase, or make profitable everything her husband gives her to benefit their family. When the woman does her job properly she will multiply or produce a return on whatever her husband gives her exponentially.

Now, a man cannot lord over his wife and force her to do this. In an effort to subdue her or make her submit he will suppress her capacity to multiply exponentially. GOD commanded the male and female to subdue the earth together. HE did not charge the man to subdue the woman. The word subdue means: under control, bondage, subjection, force, keep under, overcome, or enslave. Men don't have to engage in activities that are designed to control or dominate their wives. GOD has already dealt with this issue for us in Genesis 3:16 where HE told the woman: "and thy desire shall be to thy husband, and he shall rule over thee." If you are conducting yourself and leading her properly, submitting to you will come naturally because GOD placed that desire in her. In order to be fruitful a man must plant seeds in his wife. In order to multiply exponentially a woman cannot be suppressed or subdued mentally, spiritually, or emotionally. Otherwise, whatever she produces will be dwarfed and/or deformed.

Be Fruitful and Multiply

Iif you are going to fulfill GOD's command to be fruitful and multiply, you must first identify what you are supposed to multiply. What is the material, object, or seed that you must plant to bring to fruit or make fruitful? Your preacher will tell you that seed is money but GOD said that seed is the word of GOD. Mark 4:14 says: "The sower sows the word." The seed you sow to become fruitful is the word of GOD. The place where you sow the word of GOD to make it fruitful and multiply is in your heart or in you and your wife's spirit. Once you sow the word and begin to cultivate it in your heart it will begin to grow in your family exponentially. The word will increase from knowledge, to wisdom, to understanding.

If you explain the vision that GOD has for your life to your wife and you can you can show her how this vision will come fruition through the word of GOD, she will help you cultivate it and deliver it through her physical body. Cultivating or diligently applying the word of GOD in you and your life will cause it to multiply from fruit, to more fruit, to much fruit. Some will be able to multiply their fruit 30 fold, some 60, and some 100. GOD commanded all of us to be fruitful and multiply however our level of produce will depend on our personal level of growth in the word. Men can be fruitful or produce fruit, married men can produce more fruit, and husbands can produce much fruit. Women can produce fruit, married women can produce more fruit, and wives can produce much fruit.

Again, the result of a multiplication math problem is called: a product. The amount of product that you can produce from being fruitful and multiplying depends on whether or not you allow the power in the word of GOD that you have sown in you to work in you. Ephesians 3:20 says "Now unto him that is able to do exceeding abundantly above all that we ask or think, according to the power that worketh in us. Your product will increase exceedingly and abundantly when you have the ability to multiply on the powers level. When a couple learns to be fruitful and multiply using their GOD given power they can put ten thousand haters to flight. And this power gives them the ability to multiply wealth exponentially. You can go to my website www.WealthBuilderSeminars.com and download the audio book "There's Gold in them Heels" if you want a detailed explaination on how to make this power work in your family.

Can You be a Man Like Joseph?

"Now the birth of Jesus Christ was on this wise. When as His mother Mary was espoused to Joseph, before they came together, she was found with child of the Holy Ghost. Then Joseph her husband, being a just man, and not willing to make her a public example, was minded to put her away privately. But while he thought on these things, behold, the angel of the Lord appeared unto him in a dream, saying, Joseph, you son of David, fear not to take unto you Mary your wife: for that which is conceived in her is of the Holy Ghost. And she shall bring forth a son, and you shall call His name JESUS: for He shall save his people from their sins… Then Joseph being raised from sleep did as the angel of the Lord had bidden him, and took unto him his wife (Matthew 1:1825)."

Brothers, if a woman that you were engaged to be married to came and told you that she was pregnant, and she said the Holy Spirit did it, what would you do? In the days of Mary and Joseph, by Jewish law, Joseph had the right to have Mary stoned to death. Would you have been so hurt and upset that you would have had her stoned in public immediately? Or would you have been like Joseph and try to think about how to put this matter to rest privately?

The fact that Joseph didn't have her stoned to death immediately reveals something about his heart and character as a man. It also provides some insight into why

Can You be a Man Like Joseph?

GOD selected Joseph to raise Jesus. What kind of man would you have to be for GOD to choose 'vyou to raise HIS only begotten Son? We know that a boy will take on some of the qualities, characteristics, values, and beliefs of the man that raises him. It is only natural for a boy to look up to his daddy and allow that man to guide him into his destiny.

If GOD decided to have Jesus' return come through a woman again, do you think that HE could trust you to raise Jesus? Could GOD depend on you to see that HIS Son was guided into the completion and fulfillment of his destiny to be the Savior of all humanity?

As far as we know, Joseph had never had an angel speak to him before this incident. Yet, we see that he was obviously faithful in addition to being a just man because he did exactly what the angel instructed him to do. There was no hesitation or mental reservation; he simply got up and took responsibility for the baby and his mommy. It appears to me that responsibility or "response ability" was another quality in Joseph's character that led GOD to choose him. He had response ability or the ability to respond properly in each situation. Instead of reacting wildly, he thought to put Mary away privately. Rather than abandoning Mary and her baby, and be done, he decided to take care of her and her son.

"And when they were departed, behold, the angel of the Lord appeared to Joseph in a dream, saying, arise, and take the young child and His mother, and flee into Egypt, and be you there until I bring you word: for Herod will seek the young child to destroy Him (Matthew 2:13)."

"But when Herod was dead, behold, an angel of the Lord appeared in a dream to Joseph in Egypt, saying, arise, and take the young child and His mother, and go into the land of Israel: for they are dead which sought the young child's life (Matthew 2:1920)."

These two scenes are strange in light of how men would normally conduct ourselves in this situation. Mothers today who are married to a man that is not their child's father would want to make decisions about what should be done to protect her son. They don't trust the man to make those decisions because, after all, he is not the boy's real daddy so (in her mind) he couldn't possibly love "her" son as much as she does. However, this should be a lesson to all liberated women. The child may be your baby but if you are married, GOD intends for your baby to be your husband's responsibility. While he may not be they boy's natural father, as your husband he is that boy's daddy. Therefore, GOD is not going to instruct you on what to do with the child. HE is going to tell your husband. This is crucial because men have the responsibility to guide children into their destiny. A woman can nurture and guide a child to grow up righteously but the child needs a daddy to guide him or her into their GOD ordained destiny.

Now, there is something else strange in these verses related to Joseph. We can surmise from the context as to the type of man he was but the Bible doesn't really tell us much about him. Since I couldn't find much in the Bible about Joseph I began searching historical records and zip, nada, nothing much there either. Then I finally realized why the Bible didn't tell us much about Joseph. It's because it tells you everything about Jesus. You see, a good man hides his life in the life of his son, so that to know the son is to know the father (read John 8:19). This is the same reason the Bible doesn't tell us much specifically about GOD. The Bible teaches us more about the faith, character, and integrity of Jesus than it does about GOD. Since we know all of the characteristics and qualities of Jesus, we can know the attributes of His Father because GOD breathed or inspired HIS life into HIS Son.

"Now after the death of Moses the servant of the LORD it came to pass that the LORD spoke unto Joshua the son of Nun... (Joshua 1:1)"

Joshua is the first book of prophecy that teaches us about the coming of Jesus. Joshua and Nun are merely an allegory for GOD and Jesus. The book of Joshua constantly refers to him as the son of Nun. Yet, it never tells you anything about Nun. But that is because it told you all about Joshua. Nun was a faithful father. A faithful father hides his life in his son's life so that the son represents or re/presents the father to the world wherever he goes. We know all about Nun because we heard all about Joshua. We know all about GOD because we heard all about Jesus. Similarly, the world should be able to learn everything they need to know about you once they have heard all about your children.

Whenever Jesus' name is called, most of us begin to think about the impact that GOD has had in our lives. We love Jesus but we immediately begin to give GOD credit. When your name is called what impact will people see in their lives as a result of the children you gave birth to? GOD intended for every father to be like Jesus Christ and for every child to be like his or her dad. Then, every man, woman, boy or girl would know who Jesus is, have a life worthy of emulating, and grow into the image and likeness of Jesus. If men handle our responsibility faithfully and guide our children into their GOD ordained destiny, the impact of their lives will resonate throughout the earth into eternity.

The way GOD measures a man is in whether or not he led his wife and children to reach their GOD ordained destiny. A husband and/or dad is responsible for what the people he is given charge over do or don't do (read Hosea 4:412). It does not take a special type of man to lead his family to into their destiny. It simply takes a man who has obtained victory over himself and who will yield himself to the knowledge and wisdom of GOD in order to complete this responsibility successfully.

Joseph was the type of man who yielded himself to the wisdom and knowledge of GOD. This is another reason GOD selected him to be the dad, caretaker, and administrator of the Savior. Joseph proved that he would be led of GOD and demonstrated that he was a man of wisdom in so much as he did what GOD instructed him to do in order to keep Herod from killing his son. If Joseph had not done what GOD instructed him to do, Jesus would not have lived to reach his GOD ordained destiny. Jesus needed Joseph to fulfill his created purpose and to take on the responsibilities of being his daddy which is to guide, guard, and govern; direct, correct, and protect Him as a baby so that He could reach His GOD ordained destiny. Every time we thank GOD for Jesus we should also give HIM thanks for Joseph.

Section III
IN-FORMATION
Transformation of the Heart and Mind

Section III

The Truth about Perfection

"And HE gave some apostles; and some prophets; and some evangelists; and some pastors and teachers; For the perfecting of the saints, for the work of the ministry, for the edifying of the body of Christ: Till we all come in the unity of the faith, and of the knowledge of the Son of GOD, unto a perfect man, unto the measure of the stature of the fullness of Christ... But speaking the truth in love, may grow up into Him IN ALL THINGS, which is the head, even Christ (Ephesians 4:1113 & 15)."

The key to growing up into the measure and stature of the fulness of Christ is in understanding perfection. Many people believe the Biblical definition of perfection is maturity. Studying the word "perfect" thoroughly in the Hebrew and Greek lexicons will not yield the word "mature" in any of their translations. The word "perfect" in the above scripture is translated from the Greek word "teleios" which has three meanings: 1) complete in growth; or 2) complete in mental and moral character. The third definition from Greek translates into the English phrase: "of full age". It has a dual reference in terms of being measured in the stature of the fullness of Jesus Christ or to the fulness of time. The word "age" comes from the Greek word "eon" which means time. Whenever the Bible uses the phrase "it came to pass", it can be substituted for the phrase "in the fullness of time" or once the time for this season was up. The word "perfecting" means "in the process of being completely furnished". That is, being engaged in doing all that one needs to do, in order to do, that which he was assigned to do.

How did the word "mature" become the definition of the word perfect in the minds of those who seek to preach and teach the word of GOD? The answer to that question is unclear but their conclusion is wrong. Reading a false definition into a verse where one finds the word perfect causes men to both mistranslate and misinterpret scripture, which leads to improper conclusions. GOD intended for every man to become perfect or perfected in Christ Jesus so that we can be as Jesus is.

"Let this mind be in you, which was also in Christ Jesus, who, being in the form of GOD, thought it not robbery to be equal with GOD (Philippians 2:56)."

"…But we have the mind of Christ (1 Corinthians 2:16)."

"And be not conformed to this world: but be ye transformed by the renewing of your mind, that ye may prove what is that good, acceptable and perfect will of GOD (Romans 12:2)."

"Whereof I am made a minister according to the dispensation of GOD, which is given to me for you, to fulfill the word of GOD; Even the mystery which hath been hid from ages and from generations, but now [not some time in the future] is manifest to his saints. To whom GOD would make known what is the riches of the glory of this mystery among the Gentiles; which is Christ in you, the hope of glory: Whom we preach, warning every man, and teaching every man in all wisdom [to know and do what GOD said]; that we may present every man PERFECT in Christ Jesus (Ephesians 1:2528)."

The mere suggestion that we can be perfect as Jesus is causes religious people to bust a blood vessel in rage. They portend that they trying to defend His honor when they are actually trying to thwart His message. Jesus is trying to teach us Himself that we can escape or overcome the sin that is in the world through the lust of the flesh (read 2 Peter 1:34) by GOD's divine power. And that we can be partakers of GOD's divine nature through the knowledge of Him or through the knowledge of the word of GOD and become complete, fulfilled, or perfected in Him. But religious people argue that this is impossible. Therefore, we must break free from the doctrines of religious people so that we can learn the truth of the word, renew our minds, grow up into perfection in Christ, and become as He is.

"Beloved, NOW are we the sons of GOD, and it doth not yet appear what we shall be: but we know that, when He shall appear, we shall be like Him; for we shall see Him as He is. And every man that hath this hope in him purifies himself, even as he is pure (1 John 3:23)."

The Truth about Perfection

Jesus admonished us in Matthew 5:48 to be perfect even as GOD is perfect. He said in Luke 6:40 that everyone who is perfect shall be as GOD. Jesus prayed in John 17:21-23 that we would be perfect in one with Him as He is perfect in one with GOD. While religious people think they are doing the will of GOD, they are actually doing the work of satan. They are defying the word of GOD by withholding the truth about perfection from HIS people. Most of the rejection of the perfection of man in the body comes out of teaching from Old Testament Law. The scriptures clearly show us that we can not be made perfect under The Law. However, we can be made perfect by grace, which is the power of GOD operating on behalf of the believer. See Hebrews 7:19-28 and 1 Peter 5:10.

The 7 Step Progression of Sin

"And let us consider one another to provoke unto love and to good works: not forsaking the assembling of ourselves together, as the manner of some is; but exhorting one another: and so much the more, as ye see the day approaching. For if we sin wilfully after that we have received the knowledge of the truth, there remaineth no more sacrifice for sins (Hebrews 10:2426)."

One of the reasons why men and women of GOD (who have made the confession of salvation) continue to vacillate in and out of sin is we have never been taught how to overcome sin. In the 10th chapter of the book of Hebrews GOD is trying to teach us how to overcome sin. However, we never learned how to overcome sin because preachers twisted verse 25 of Hebrews 10 to deceive us into believing that it is a mandate from GOD that we must "go" to church. If you put verse 25 back into context by reading chapter 10 in its entirety, you will see that verse is NOT talking about and has NOTHING to do with "going" to church. The word "ourselves" appeared in the original text as "our selves". For whatever reason the translators made those two words one word which changed the meaning of the verse.

Every man is a tripartite being comprised of a mind, body, and spirit. These are three separate entities. They are our three selves: a mind self, a body self and a spirit self.

The 7 Step Progression of Sin

Whenever these three selves are in conflict or cannot agree it leads men to fall easily to sin. This is what the Apostle Paul meant when he said in Romans 7:15: "For that which I do I allow not: for what I would, that do I not; butwhat I hate, that do I." His mind and body were in conflict therefore he knew what to do but sometimes he just failed to do it. He knew what not to do but sometimes he did it anyway and he hated it. Men get caught up in sin when our "selves" come into conflict. We know what not to do yet we do it anyway. This is why Hebrews 10:25 is admonishing us to "forsake not" or don't fail to assemble our "selves" together or bring them out of conflict and into agreement so that we can have the power to overcome sin.

Brothers, we were all born in sin and shaped in iniquity therefore the penchant for sin is always present within us. This is why we must be born again. Those who refuse to become born again must understand that there are 5 phases of sin: presence, power, practice, process, and penalty. There are 7 steps in the process that ultimately leads to the penalty which is death. Hosea 4:6 says: my people are destroyed for a lack of knowledge. GOD also said in that verse: if you reject knowledge I will reject you and your children too. It would be wise then, if you have no plans to be born again, to receive this information so that you can understand sin and be equipped with the knowledge you need to make a wise decision.

Since we were all born in sin it can be present in you but there is no penalty for sin if you don't put it into practice. The problem we have is we live in a world that is governed by satan where there is always a power source of sin that causes it to activate or come alive and lead you to put it into practice. This can be compared to a car battery which is the car's power source. It needs that power to get turned on. But once the car is running you can totally remove the battery and the car will continue to run. The presence of sin in you does not automatically make contact with the power source that turns it on. You have to do something or put yourself in position to make contact. When it does make contact it does not always get turned on right away. Some form of pressure is the key that causes you to make contact with the power that activates sin. This is similar to when you turn a key to start your car's engine. You have to hold the key down until the engine turns on. Then the power is transferred over to the alternator or the car's power generator. Now the car will run on its own or under its own power.

Once the presence of sin is activated by pressure and power you will begin to practice sin. Just as with the car you can now remove the source of power and the sin will begin to pressure you to practice it under its own power. This is similar to what happens to a young boy who gets molested by a man. The man was the power source that activated sin. The man can be separated from the boy but the sin has been activated in him. Therefore, he will be pressured by the sin to continue to practice it on his own.

Men get involved in three types of deal: the ordeal, the ideal, and let's make a deal. The ideal is what GOD wants for your life. Let's make a deal is the promise you make to

GOD if HE will let you do what you want with your life. The ordeal is the misery you have to go through as a result of doing what you want to do instead of what GOD would have you to do. The ordeal, or the product of doing what you want to do, causes you to enter into the 7 step process of sin which are: Observation, Stimulation, Admiration, Experimentation, Participation, Consummation and Reprobation.

The seven step process of sin begins with observation. A man starts the descent into reprobation by seeing the object of his lust. He becomes stimulated by what he sees and his flesh becomes activated at the thought of indulging in the object of their lust. At this point he begins to admire people who participate in that sin and he begins to gain a mental acceptance of fulfilling the lust. He convinces his "selves" that there is nothing wrong because everybody is doing it. That is the point where he gets into experimentation by deciding to "try it just once". We convince ourselves to try it by saying it will only be one time but it never turns out to be just once. The fifth step in the process is participation where we begin to engage in the lust more and more often. The sixth step is consummation wherein the lust for that desire is beginning to consume us. Our hearts or thoughts and mind are consumed by it. We plan our activities around it and we select our friends based on it. The seventh or final step in the process of sin is reprobation where we lose the power or ability to make a godly choice and quit.

The 7 Step Progression of Sin

When a man becomes reprobate, he is cut off from the True and Living GOD and dies a spiritual death. This is why it is so difficult to overcome addiction. Lust fights the flesh to make it long for what it is addicted to even though the person may be weary of being addicted. The person knows what they are doing is contrary to the will of GOD and their own will for their lives. However, they left GOD in pursuit of lust and sin. Consequently, the activity or thing a man is lusting for becomes his GOD. GOD releases him, then, to lasciviousness or the uncontrolled lust of his flesh. Therefore, it will take an extreme circumstance, severe trauma, or hitting "rock bottom" to cause the person to turn from their lust and cry out to GOD. Unless a person hits rock bottom and determines on their own that they need help from GOD to be free, you and I will waste our time, energy, and resources trying to help them before then. At this point, the man is spiritually dead and is headed toward physical death. Spiritual death ultimately leads to physical death. People who have become reprobate are like those who live the so called "fast life". Sin is called the fast life because it will end your life fast (read Romans 8:13).

Reprobation is one level of the penalty for sin but then comes death which is the ultimate penalty. We cannot lie to our children and simply tell them that sin is bad. We must let them know that initially sin is fun and it feels good. It makes us believe that everybody does it so nobody should judge but that is the lure or the trap. And we have to make them see clearly that the penalty of sin and the 7 step process that leads to the ultimate penalty which is just like taking that first hit of crack. The party where you took the first hit was fun, the people were fun to hang with, and that first hit made you feel good. Everybody there was doing it and nobody was judging anybody. But crack addiction will move you through the process of sin quickly to the point where you won't be able to make the godly choice to quit. However, if you don't cry out to GOD and get HIS help to quit, it will lead to death.

When you get a chance compare Romans 10 to Hebrews 10 and you will see that GOD and Jesus were admonishing us to assemble or get our "selves" together so that we can receive their offering which is something better than sin.

Voice of GOD vs. Voice of Satan

"And he said, go forth, and stand upon the mount before the Lord. And, behold, the Lord passed by, and a great and strong wind rent the mountains, and brake in pieces the rocks before the Lord; but the Lord was not in the wind: and after the wind an earthquake; but the Lord was not in the earthquake: and after the earthquake a fire; but the Lord was not in the fire: and after the fire a still small voice. And it was so, when Elijah heard it, that he wrapped his face in his mantle, and went out, and stood in the entering in of the cave. And, behold, there came a voice unto him, and said, what doest thou here, Elijah (1 Kings 19:1113)?"

There is a reason GOD placed you here. There is a purpose that HE wants you to fulfill that will benefit mankind before you exit this planet. That job or assignment is unique to the knowledge, gifts, talents, and abilities that HE placed in you when you were born. It is a job that nobody can do but you.

Therefore, whenever GOD speaks to you it will be pertaining to something that HE wants you to do. With GOD everything is always about going and doing. This is why one of the pieces of armor in the whole armor of GOD is foot wear (Ephesians 6:12) or having your feet shod with the preparation of the gospel of peace. If you analyze the name of GOD you will notice that two thirds of HIS name spelled forward is GO and two thirds of HIS name spelled

Voice of GOD vs. Voice of Satan

backward is DO. When GOD gives you a command to GO and DO that is a GOD Ordained Divine Opportunity to achieve glory. All of the heroes in the Hebrews 11 hall of fame of faith obtained glory because GOD said go and do, and by faith they went and did.

Now, we have five voices that we have to contend with on a daily basis that are ALL trying to control what we do and where we go. Those voices are: the voice of our spirit, the voice of our mind, the voice of our body (when you want a cookie that is your body speaking), the voice of GOD, and the voice of the devil who always tries to pretend that he is GOD. Therefore, we must know how to tell the difference between satan's voice and the voice of GOD.

When the voice of GOD is heard outside of us is thunderous, sounds like rushing rivers, and is powerful. Once you get a chance read: John 12:2829, Ezekiel 43:2, and Psalms 29:4 and you will see what I mean. Additionally, GOD's voice will always be in concert and never in conflict with HIS word. The devil's voice is always deceiving, tempting, and tormenting. Read Matthew chapter 4, Genesis 3, and Mark chapters 5 and 9. There you will see that the devil will always try to use the word in an effort to make us believe that he is GOD speaking but the word he speaks will always be a twisted version of GOD's word.

Whenever GOD speaks to us from the inside HE is actually speaking through the Holy Spirit. The Holy Spirit is the feminine aspect of the Triune GODHEAD [man,

Voice of GOD vs. Voice of Satan

woman and child; father, mother and son]. Therefore, it comes up in a still or quiet manner that sounds like a harmonious or melodic tone. Until our body is made a living sacrifice unto GOD whenever we hear the voice of GOD our inclination is to go in the opposite direction; to run and hide. This is why after something bad happened you said: something told me to or something told me not to. That something was the voice of GOD via the Holy Spirit trying to guide, direct, and protect you but you chose to do the opposite of what HE said to do.

Our instinct to go in the opposite direction is the reason I believe GOD chooses to speak to us quietly and melodically. This reminds me of a teacher I had in high school. Whenever he tried to give us personal advice and we didn't agree he would respond in a quiet musical tone by saying: "allllriiiight sucka!" At the end of the day we would find out that he was right and would have to do what he said anyway. I believe, therefore, that GOD speaks using harmony or the musical scale to lead us into harmony or agreement with HIS will as well as to teach us a lesson.

The musical scale is: do, re, me, fa, so, la, ti, do. Now, the first note is pronounced doe but it is actually do because everything that GOD says is an instruction to go and do. Since we tend to run in an opposite direction from what GOD said to do we usually find our self in difficulty and eventually have to go back to the point where we disobeyed GOD and do what HE told us to "do".

We end up going back up the musical scale to the beginning but only after reaching the end of the scale and realizing we ran into the same instruction: do! We never realized that at the beginning and the end of the music scale you will find the same command from GOD: "do". You can run and hide but at the end of the day you will always have to "do" what GOD said. There is power, riches, and glory or fulfillment waiting for us if we would just do whatever GOD gave us an assignment to complete or fulfill.

Colossians 1:18-19 says: "And He [Jesus] is the head of the body, the church: who is the beginning, the firstborn from the dead; that in all things He might have the preeminence (which translated from the Greek word "proteuo" means first or first example). For it pleased the Father that in Him should all fullness dwell."

You see, GOD made Jesus after HIS likeness to provide us with an example of what HE wanted us to be like. Then GOD sent Jesus here to do various exploits to be an example of what HE expects us to do. So, whatever we have seen Jesus do in the word it is an example to show us what we can do in the world.

What we can do in, by, or through Christ Jesus is utilize His power to cast out demons, heal the sick, and mend the broken hearted. We can control our environment, just as Jesus controlled the wind and the waves of the sea. Just as Jesus walked on the water and Peter followed after, we can do this and more if we only have the faith to believe that we can.

Voice of GOD vs. Voice of Satan

Psalms 121:12 says: "I will lift up my eyes unto the hills from whence comes my help. My help comes from the LORD."

As a child of GOD you cannot enjoy the full rights and benefits of the New Covenant until you go through the Romans 12:12 process and come into the measure and stature of the fullness of Christ Jesus. GOD has given you an opportunity to receive your rights and benefits through the system of the Kingdom of GOD. Now, you have to go in and possess them. As GOD told the children of Israel, I have given you the Promised Land now you have to take possession of it. The devil and his disciples have found a way to wall you off from your inheritance to keep you from taking it. This is why Jesus said: the Kingdom of GOD suffers violence and the violent take it by force. GOD will show you how to fight the devil and win, like HE did with Joshua at the battle of Jericho. But GOD's way is not our way so HE is going to tell you to do something that is weird but if you just do what HE said to do that wall will fall flat for you.

"And the Lord said unto Joshua, see, I have given into thine hand Jericho, and the king thereof, and the mighty men of valor. And ye shall compass the city, all ye men of war, and go round about the city once. Thus shalt thou do six days. And seven priests shall bear before the ark seven trumpets of rams' horns: and the seventh day ye shall compass the city seven times, and the priests shall blow with the trumpets. And it shall come to pass, that when they make a long blast with the ram's horn, and when ye hear the sound of the trumpet, all the people shall shout with a great shout; and the wall of the city shall fall down flat, and the people shall ascend up every man straight before him (Joshua 6:25)."

GOD told Joshua and the men of Israel to go and do something that seemed weird and useless in the natural so that HE could deliver a supernatural result. In order for GOD to deliver supernatural blessings HE needs us to give HIM permission to act on our behalf by being in agreement or acting in obedience to HIS word. Joshua and the men of Israel went and did what GOD said and they were able to receive what HE had promised.

The walls of Jericho were wide enough for houses to sit on top and for chariots to ride back and forth on it like a two lane street. Rahab the harlot's house was on top of the wall. This is why she was able to let Joshua's spies down the wall through her back window to escape without being seen. This tells you the phrase "fell flat" does not mean the walls fell over on their side because they would still be too high for every man to simply walk straight before him to take the city. Instead of walking straight ahead they would have had to climb up about 20 yards of wall. The phrase fell flat is how a building falls that is taken down by controlled demolition. It collapses flat on its own footprint. When the walls of Jericho fell they simply dropped straight down below the ground. You can go there today and see them submerged below the dirt.

The devil and his disciples have the wealth that GOD laid up for you walled off. Therefore, you will have to go in and take possession of it. If you go and do whatever GOD tells you to do, HE will make that wall collapse for you and then you can walk straight in and take it by force.

Voice of GOD vs. Voice of Satan

Receive the Gifts of the Holy Spirit

"...the manifestation of the Spirit is given to every man to profit withal for to one is given by the Spirit the word of wisdom; to another the word of knowledge by the same Spirit; to another faith by the same Spirit; to another the gifts of healing by the same Spirit; to another the working of miracles; to another prophecy; to another discerning of spirits; to another divers kinds of tongues; to another the interpretation of tongues: but all these worketh that one and the selfsame Spirit, dividing to every man severally as HE will (1 Corinthians 12:711)."

"...the fruit of the Spirit is love, joy, peace, longsuffering, gentleness, goodness, faith, meekness, and temperance: against such there is no law (Galatians 5:2223)."

"...unto every one of us is given grace [or the power of GOD to work on our behalf] according to the measure of the gift of Christ. Wherefore He said when He ascended up on high, He led captivity captive, and gave gifts unto men... and He gave some, apostles; and some, prophets; and some, evangelists; and some, pastors and teachers; for the perfecting of the saints, for the work of the ministry, for the edifying of the body of Christ: till we all come in the unity of the faith, and of the knowledge of the Son of GOD, unto a perfect man, unto the measure of the stature of the fulness of Christ: that we henceforth be no more children, tossed to and fro, and carried about with every wind of doctrine, by the sleight of men, and cunning craftiness, whereby they lie in wait to deceive (Ephesians 4:714)."

"Now there are diversities of gifts, but the same Spirit. And there are differences of administrations but the same Lord. And there are diversities of operations [or manifestations] but it is the same GOD that works all in all (1 Corinthians 12:46)."

Notice the word says that GOD gives the gifts of the Holy Spirit to EVERY man so he can profit or use them to be productive in Christ Jesus. It does NOT say that the gifts of the Holy Spirit are only given to paostors or those in church leadership. It also says that GOD will give EVERY man several of these gifts as HE wills or deems it necessary. So, why is GOD dispensing the gifts of the Holy Spirit to every man? It's because HE intended for every man to be the king and priest of his home. Every man needs the gifts of the Holy Spirit manifesting in his life so that his wife and children will be motivated to follow him as he is following Christ Jesus. His family also needs to see the fruits of the Spirit manifesting in him so they will know that he has integrity in Christ Jesus, there will be no turning away, and they won't be led astray.

"But the anointing which ye have received of him abideth in you, and ye need not that any man teach you: but as the same anointing teacheth you of all things, and is truth, and is no lie, and even as it hath taught you, ye shall abide in him (1 John 2:27)."

"Study to show thyself approved unto GOD, a workman that needeth not to be ashamed, rightly dividing the word of truth (2 Timothy 2:15)."

Anyone who has been going to church for a substantial length of time knows that everyone who claims to be called to preach in the pulpit was not actually called. There are those who have gone that were not sent; some were called but some just went. This is why their teaching does not really convey the truth of the word of GOD. This is why their "GOD is getting ready to, going to, and about to bless you propheises never come true. They are trying to teach the word of GOD without the anointing or guidance of one who occupies the 5 fold ministry off of Teacher. No man who is operating in the 5 fold ministry Office of Pastor can claim to also have the anointing that belongs to the 5 fold ministry Office of Teacher.

There is a gift of wisdom and a gift of a word of knowledge but there is NO gift of teaching. The Holy Spirit provides the unique anointing of the teacher to those who operate in the Office of Teacher. There is NO place in the word that says GOD calls men to operate in "several" 5 fold ministry offices. Each office is a separate administration and a separate operation. However, each office is given a special power or anointing that when combined with the other offices creates a unique power to overcome and/or defeat the devil. As a pastor you can receive the gifts of wisdom and/or the word of knowledge to use to help you lead people to come into Christ Jesus. But, after you have led them to come to Christ Jesus you must turn them over to someone who is anointed in the Office of Teacher. The Teacher will then provide them with instruction on how to walk in, walk with, and operate through Christ Jesus. Pastors are NOT anointed to do this which is why the average Christian is powerless.

Most Christians are trying hard to live their lives by the word but it does not work for the most part because the word they received by religious doctrine and tradition is not true. The word they receive in church may be truly stated but it is not truth. Thus, they struggle to break free from satanic attack and the sin that so easily beset them because only the truth makes you free. Only the truth makes the devil flee. The devil took the truth that we need to make him flee and hid it in false doctrine and tradition. Then, he made it almost impossible for anyone to teach us the truth because he attached his false doctrine to something very sentimental such as a parent, grandparent, or favorite preacher. We love them and strongly believe they would never teach us anything wrong so we hold on to their false doctrine. The problem is they didn't know what they were taught wasn't true. Therefore, they were sincere when they taught you that false doctrine in love but they were sincerely wrong.

In order to have the power to make the devil flee, fulfill our created purpose, and receive glory we must study diligently to learn the truth about three important attributes of GOD. Those attributes are abstract in the minds of most Christians due to false doctrine. The three most important attributes of GOD are: faith, grace, and truth. Again, the devil has hidden the truth about what faith and grace actually are in false doctrine. Ergo, the average Christian has more faith in a GPS to lead them to a destination on the road than they do in the Holy Spirit to lead them to their destiny in life. The average Christian is more likely to step out on the word of a bus schedule than they are to step out on the words in the Bible. That is because the word they received through false doctrine does not work. The bus will show up at the place and time the schedule said it would. But the promises in the Bible don't ever seem to appear as the preacher said they would.

Up until now Christians have been tricked into using the tools of anger and indignation to try to defeat the devil but those are his weapons. Preachers always try to lead you to say things like: "the devil is a lie!" but please read 2 Peter 2:11 and Jude 1:9 right now and read them in context. You can't cast out the devil with the devil. If the devil was superman, faith, grace, and truth would be his kryptonite. Therefore, every man must allow the Holy Spirit to be their teacher. The Holy Spirit will gift or grace you with the truth and power that you need to defeat the devil.

John 8:32 says: You shall know the truth and the truth shall MAKE you free. Ask yourself are you truly free spiritually, emotionally, and financially? Those who have not been given over to a strong delusion will freely admit that they are not free especially not financially. Jesus said if you know the truth the truth shall make (not set) you free. If the word you have been receiving in your church was true, why are you not free yet? The word "know" in this verse means to have intimate contact. When you have intimate contact with the truth the truth will make you totally free. Notice that verse says the truth shall make you free when just about everyone you know, including your favorite preacher, quotes that verse saying: the truth shall SET you free. There is a major difference between the words make and set.

In times of slavery there were free Black people. They were free because they were born free. There was a law that prohibited a freeborn Black person from being made a slave. The man who made a freeborn Black person a slave could go to prison. Those Black people remained free of slavery's captivity because they were made or born free. A slave master could set a slave free but if he lost the papers that proved he was free, he could be taken back into captivity. When you are set free by your preacher you can be taken back into captivity by the devil. This is what many Christians call "back sliding". The reason they backslide is because they never knew the truth. However, when you are made free you can never be taken captive involuntarily. Jesus said: I am the way, the truth, and the life. Once you have intimate contact with the truth or have Christ IN you who IS the truth, the devil cannot capture you physically, mentally, emotionally, spiritually or financially because you are made free in, by, or through Christ Jesus.

The Question of a Man's Covering

"But I would have you know that the head of every man is Christ; and the head of the woman is the man; and the head of Christ is GOD (1 Corinthians 11:3)."

What is a "spiritual coverying"? Frankly, I can't answer that question, in terms of the way the word is being used in church. Preachers describe a covering as "one who is in authority over or has submited themselves to their authority for the purpose of giving or receiving spiritual, professional, and personal guidance and direction." My problem is, I can't find the word "covering" being used with that definition in that manner in the Bible. The charismatic influenced preachers who preach the prosperity gospel say it is unscriptural not to have a covering. That is, some other man in authority over you. However, I can not find in the Bible where any man or woman of GOD made that assertion.

There are some references where we are being reminded to operate within the bounds of civil or governmental authority, basically to obey civil law. But I find no scripture where any man is commanded or remanded to have or keep another man in authority or as a "covering" over them. To be respectful I say that I can't find a scripture. However, the blunt truth is there is none in the Bible. The direct opposite of what charismatic or prosperity preachers teach is in the Bible. Man covering man is something those preachers crafted in the carnality of their own minds in order to gain and maintain control over other men and essentially turn them into a mangina or a female man.

The objective is to get men to relinquish authority over what GOD gave them authority over (like satan did with Adam) including their wives, their children, and their finances. This is just as offensive to GOD as Adam yielding to satan or as Esau giving up his birthright (something of value) for something desired. The word says GOD hated Esau for doing that. In Matthew 4:8-9 satan tried to get Jesus to allow him to be His covering (in authority over Him) instead of GOD. Do you think GOD would have been happy with Jesus if He put Satan between himself and GOD? No! Likewise, GOD is not happy with you when you put satan or a man who is a defacto representative of satan between yourself and HIM. Let's see what the Apostle Paul says about man being a covering for other men in 1 Corinthians 11:3-16.

"But I would have you know that the head of every man is Christ; and the head of the woman is the man; and the head of Christ is GOD."

Paul is clearly saying that the head or the one who is supposed to "cover" or be in authority over every man is Christ. He is bluntly stating in a matter of fact way "I, as a spiritual leader, am not your head or covering". He also said that the head of the woman (meaning the married

The Question of a Man's Covering

woman) is the man or her husband. A married woman should not have a preacher or some man other than her own husband in authority over her (See Ephesians 5:2224, Colossians 3:18, Titus 2:5 and 1 Peter 3:1). An unmarried woman's head or covering is her father. The father remains in authority over her until he passes authority over her to her husband when he gives her away at her wedding. Next, Paul says the head, covering, or the one in authority over Christ is GOD.

"Every man praying or prophesying having his head covered dishonoreth his head. But every [married] woman that prayeth or prophesieth with her head uncovered dishonoreth her head: for that is even all one as [the same as] if she were shaven."

I wish Paul had not interjected the "hair" analogy in this teaching because it makes the issue in modern day society take a side issue. Anyway, praying is talking to GOD and prophesying is speaking on behalf of GOD. Paul just told us that the head of man is Christ and the head of the woman is man. Now, he is saying that when a man tries to talk to GOD or speak on behalf of GOD (preacher) with another man covering or in authority over him, that man dishonors Christ Jesus. It would stand to reason then that when a woman tries to talk to GOD or speak on behalf of GOD with a preacher or some man other than her husband covering or in authority over her, she dishonors her husband.

However, Paul is actually talking specifically here about the woman attempting to talk to GOD or speak on HIS behalf without being under the authority of her husband. That is, knowingly being out of line or in disagreement with what her husband has prayed or prophesied. Paul is saying that she might as well be a man since she is trying to act like one. Remember, as we go through these verses of 1 Corinthians 11, that Paul is using shaving or references to hair as an analogy given that hair is a type of covering or veil for the head. Jesus is a symbolic representative of the veil of the temple. As such, He is a symbolic veil for the man whereas the man is a symbolic veil for the woman.

"For if the woman be not covered, let her also be shorn: but if it be a shame for a woman to be shorn or shaven, let her be covered."

Paul says, if the woman does not want to be covered, veiled, or under the authority of her husband, then let her also shave her head. But, if it is shameful for a woman to have a shaved head then she needs some type of scarf or hat to cover her head. Unlike today, with women trying to do everything men do, it was a shame for a woman to have a bald or shaved head in Paul's day. The point Paul is trying to make here is NOT about hair. It is teach us that a man and woman are to be in order and agreement when they go before GOD if they expect HIM to honor their prayers or to reveal the prophesy for their lives. GOD established an order for husbands and wives in HIS word and HE expects them to be in that order if what HE promised for families is going to work for them. GOD intended for husbands and wives to be as one or to act in concert as if they are one. It is offensive to GOD when the husband comes to pray for something and his wife prays for the direct opposite.

"For a man indeed ought not to cover his head, forasmuch as he is the image and glory of GOD: but the woman is the glory of the man."

Now, if you said what Paul just said, the average preacher would accuse you of being blasphemous and the average feminist would accuse you of being chauvinist. He said that a man must not or has no need to have another man cover his head or be in authority over him because he is the image and glory of GOD. It does not seem to click in the minds of most preachers that when GOD said that HE made man in HIS image and after HIS likeness, HE was telling us that HE made man to both look like and to act like HIM! A child could be the spitting image of his father, but act or have a lot of ways like his mother. That is what image and likeness means.

In Psalm 82:6 GOD said "I have said, Ye are GODs; and all of you are children of the most High." Jesus repeated GOD's declaration in John 10:34 "Is it not written in your word, I said, Ye are GODs?" He also prayed in John 17:22 that we would be one with Him as He is one with the Father. Then, Paul says in Philippians 2:56 "Let this mind be in you, which was also in Christ Jesus: Who being in the form of GOD [that is, in the image and likeness of GOD], thought it not robbery to be equal with GOD."

The Question of a Man's Covering

So, you see, we don't need another man to cover or be in authority over us when we are no longer children and become the image and likeness of GOD that HE intended us to be. The word "glory" means to hold up in high honor. The only way the world can see GOD and come to know that HE is a good and faithful Father is through us. When we be as HE is, living and moving in HIS image and likeness, walking illustrations of HIS faithfulness and goodness, the world will see GOD through us and hold HIM up in high honor. The same thing occurs when a wife is a walking illustration of her husband's faithfulness and goodness. She brings glory and honor to his name as the world observes her.

"For the man is not of [that is, did not originate or derive from] the woman; but the woman of the man. Neither was the man created for the woman; but the woman for the man. For this cause ought the woman to have power on her head because of the angels."

If men try to view these verses in a chauvinistic or misogynistic manner, they will miss the blessing and power that GOD wants to lend to their lives through their wives. Likewise, if women view these verses as hatred or disdain for their individual autonomy, they will miss the blessing and power that GOD wants to lend to their lives through their husbands. Since, woman was created both out of and for man (as his help mate), the man has a responsibility to govern his wife's actions as he would govern his own. She is an extension of him and he is an extension of her. They are one. The man has a responsibility to protect the woman in the same manner as he would protect himself. Whatever happens to her happens to him. The only way the devil will be able to attack and defeat a strong man of GOD is through his wife. His love for her will cause him to submit to being bound by satan if she is in jeopardy of being hurt or killed. So Paul says, for this reason the woman ought to have power (from the Greek word "exousia" meaning authority) on her head because of the angels. The word angels in this verse comes from the Greek word "angelos" meaning the fallen angels or men who are influenced by the works of fallen angels.

In the previous verses we learned that the head of the woman is her husband. Paul is saying two things in this verse or one thing that has a double meaning. The woman needs to have a husband with power or spiritual authority in order to protect her from the devil and his demons. Conversely, because the man and the woman are one so just as he has a responsibility to guide, guard, and govern her, she is also responsible to do the same for him. Therefore, she must have spiritual authority on her head as well to protect her husband from the wiles of the devil. One of a married woman's primary duties in Christ is to protect the head of her husband as the head the family. The wife and her children are the body of the family so if the head is cut off, the body will fall.

Again, the angel in this scripture is a reference to fallen angels and to preachers who are influenced by them. In Revelation chapters 2 and 3, Jesus is addressing the angels of the churches, the leaders, or the preachers. Strong spiritual leadership has a powerful effect on women. The spiritual leadership that a woman must have in authority over her head is her husband. His job is to protect her from preachers who are corrupt, under the influence, or doing the work of fallen angels. A man's spiritual authority must be Christ not another man. A woman's husband must be her spiritual authority, not a preacher.

"Nevertheless neither is the man without the woman, neither the woman without the man, in the Lord. For as the woman is of [originated or derived from] the man, even so is the man also by [given birth through] the woman; but all things of GOD."

The Apostle Paul is saying here that the two of them are one in the Lord. One is not over the other. They each are the other. A struggle for power, position, and authority with one's spouse is really a struggle for power, position, and authority with oneself against the will of GOD. Acting in this manner is contentious and is against the express will of GOD to bring love, joy, and peace to a marriage relationship. When men don't want to become one with their wives, it is because they are actually fighting against GOD being the head of their lives. Conversely, when women fight against becoming one with their husbands, they are fighting against the order of GOD for their lives. GOD set up marriage and established its order. When a person rebels against their spouse, in actuality, they are rebelling against the order of GOD.

"Judge in yourselves: is it comely that a woman pray unto GOD uncovered?"

The word comely is translated from the Greek word "prepo", which means proper or right. The word uncovered, here, is from the Greek word "akatakaluptos" meaning unveiled. Prior to the resurrection of Jesus, man had to go behind the veil of the temple to get to GOD. Jesus has become the symbolic veil now because no man comes to the Father but by Him (John 14:6). Therefore, the covering or veil is a representation of spiritual authority. The spiritual authority of a woman is her husband. So, Paul is saying "Is it proper that a woman pray to GOD being out from under the spiritual authority of her husband?" In other words, is it right that a wife should pray to GOD for something that she knows is in opposition to what her husband is praying for? This is assuming, of course, that he is a man of GOD praying for something that is in the will of GOD for his family. In that circumstance, is it proper for a woman to go before GOD when she is in rebellion against the order of GOD?

"Doth not nature itself teach you, that if a man have long hair, it is a shame unto him? But if a woman have long hair, it is a glory to her: for her hair is given her for a covering."

This is nothing more than an analogy that Paul is using here to say that when a man is covered by another man, it is a shameful for him. That is because it places him in the position of a woman or wife and not that of a man or a husband. If you picture this sexually, the only person who should be under a man is a woman. A man who positions himself as a woman for another man will eventually lose his wife. A real woman is will want her man to be a man; not a man who acts like a woman. On the contrary, if a woman stays under the spiritual authority of her husband, it is a glory or position of honor for her. That is because her symbolic hair, veil, or husband is given to her for her spiritual protection.

Some preachers have gotten caught up in this analogy and are teaching that hair has some significance with GOD. Then, some have taught that hair in this scripture is a reference to hats or scarfs. This is why we see many women today cover their heads with a scarf before they pray and men take off their hats. However, Paul is only using the people of Corinth's concept of the relationship of hair to masculinity and femininity to illustrate a spiritual point. This has nothing whatsoever to do with pieces of handcrafted material. It has everything to do with the materiality of spiritual authority.

"But if any man seems to be contentious, we [meaning the followers of Christ] have no such custom, neither the churches of GOD."

The Question of a Man's Covering

Paul starts this chapter in verse one admonishing the people of Corinth, and by extension us today, to be followers of him as he follows Christ Jesus. Then, he reminds us in verse two to keep the ordinances or laws and rules of GOD. That is, to be mindful to maintain GOD's established order for our lives. The summation of what Paul was teaching in verses 3 through 15 is that Christ (the anointing) is the covering or spiritual authority of man and the man is the spiritual authority for the woman. The word contentious in verse 16 means to be in dispute or in strife. The word custom in this verse comes from the Greek word "sunetheia" which means: mutual habituation or usage. So, Paul concludes GOD's instruction on whether or not a man covering another man is godly by saying "If any man seems to be in dispute or in strife over what I just taught, then we followers of Christ have NO use for him and neither does the body of Christ." The doctrine of a man covering another man is nothing more than a control scheme.

The Question of a Man's Covering

About the Author

Dr William Small has helped men repair their personal and professional relationships for over 30 years. He holds a PhD in Biblical Studies and authored many books: including Strengthening the Family, Relationships: Everything You Need to Know Before You Get Married, There's Gold in Them Heels, Healing the Wounded Woman, Money DOES Grow on trees, Secrets of the Fortune 500, and more. Dr Will uses the power of excellence in relationships to lead thousands of men to become successful by helping them create a better version of themselves. He also uses this skill to produce highly proficient employees, championship sports teams, and influence drug dealers to turn their illegal operations into legitimate businesses. Dr Will conducts award winning seminars for men in the areas of domestic violence prevention and awareness, personal development, and family enrichment, along with wealth building and management. Please visit www.drwillenterprises.com for more information.

About the Author

www.ingramcontent.com/pod-product-compliance
Lightning Source LLC
Chambersburg PA
CBHW050158240426
43671CB00013B/2165